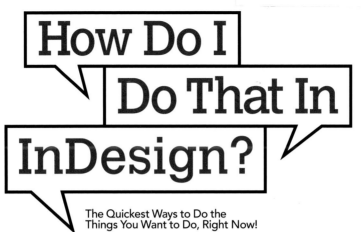

How Do I Do That In InDesign?

The Quickest Ways to Do the
Things You Want to Do, Right Now!

D1565164

Dave Clayton

Graphic Designer, KelbyOne & Photoshop World Instructor

How Do I Do That In InDesign?

The *How Do I Do That In InDesign Book* Team

SERIES EDITOR
Scott Kelby

SERIES DESIGN
Jessica Maldonado

SERIES COVER DESIGN
Jessica Maldonado

FRONT COVER DESIGN AND LAYOUT
Dave Clayton

PROJECT EDITOR
Jocelyn Howell

LAYOUT
Hespenheide Design

PROJECT MANAGER
Lisa Brazieal

MARKETING COORDINATOR
Mercedes Murray

PUBLISHED BY

Rocky Nook

Rocky Nook, Inc.
1010 B Street, Suite 350
San Rafael, CA 94901

Copyright ©2020 by Dave Clayton
For specific image credits, see page vii

ISBN: 978-1-68198-484-1

10 9 8 7 6 5 4 3 2 1

Printed and bound in the United States
Distributed in the UK and Europe by Publishers Group UK
Distributed in the U.S. and all other territories by Ingram Publisher Services
Library of Congress Control Number: 2018958254

www.kelbyone.com
www.rockynook.com
www.itsdaveclayton.com

Acknowledgments

First, my lovely family. The Claytons. All of them! This book is dedicated to my wife and children, but all the Claytons rock—aunts, uncles, cousins, and the rest of the extended family! Here's to those no longer with us, but always remembered.

Andrea: You are an absolute legend. We have four amazing children and that's because you are an amazing mum. Thank you for all your patience during the years I had to build up to days like this, and for continuing to be patient. It's appreciated more than you know! I love you.

Billy & Scott: You've grown into fine adults and are a credit to your generation and to us. You are the best big brothers to your sisters, and I am proud to be your dad!

Elise & Fleur: Elise, you are incredible in every way. Your love, your dedication, your thoughtfulness, your desire to be the best you can be. Fleur, you are amazing. You are kind, creative, loving, funny, and you make us so proud. Both of you will do great things, and you make our hearts burst every day! I love you so much!

Mum (Ann): You are our queen. I owe a lot of my early creative memories, and my love of sci-fi and television, to you! A proper East End girl who done good. Love you!

Dad (John, R.I.P.): We lost my amazing Dad on February 17th, 2018. He was an absolute legend and I owe my love of people to this great man. I miss him so much. He'd have been proud of this book! Thank you, Richard Curtis, for making *Love Actually*. Dad's only in it for seconds, but he'll be on film forever!

Alan (Big Bruv) & Jackie: You've been the best big brother I could wish for. So many unbelievable experiences in my life are thanks to you. From football matches to Dirty's gigs, The Rolling Stones, and more! Always there.

Mark (Little Bruv) & Sheelagh: You are one of the kindest and funniest guys anyone could wish to meet, almost as good as me! You're a top little brother and a great parent. Consider this your 15p repayment!

Barrie R.I.P, Paul, Rosie & Holly: Both brothers have given me wonderful nieces and nephews. I love you all.

The Garratts: Judy, Paul, John, and families. David R.I.P.

Glyn Dewis: My best mate. I could write a page about this fella. We met in 2010 thanks to Scott Kelby, and boy, what a journey we've had since in nine short years. I'm proud to share so many brilliant experiences with you, and to add author to that list is just an incredible achievement for the hard work that goes into doing what we love. Thanks, Glyn, for all the advice, friendship, and being the best roommate! Thank you, Anne, for lending me your fella!

Scott, Kalebra, Jordan & Kira Kelby: I've been associated with KelbyOne as a member since 2008 and became your Evangelist in 2009. To celebrate 10 years of friendship with this book is just a huge "pinch me" moment. Thank you for taking time on that grey day in London on October 14th, 2010, and for introducing me to Glyn. Life changing! Thank you for every opportunity you have given me, for pushing me and believing in me, and for allowing me to create content for you. Thank you for taking me into your family and being a great friend.

Alan & Nadra Hess: Thank you for allowing me to be part of your lives. It means a lot to me and mine and I hope we get to add many more amazing memories to the ones we already have! Miss my dogs!

Aaron Blaise: What can I say, one of my most favorite human beings, a creative soul, a generous heart, an incredible talent. I'm so glad we met you when we did. The best of times in your company! More memories to make.

Scott Cowlin & Ted Waitt (Rocky Nook): If I was ever going to write a book, it would only ever be with you. You are the best in the business, I just love you guys! You know how I feel, as I say it enough, but thanks for all the opportunities you've afforded me to this point. Also thanks to Mercedes, Lisa, and the whole RN book team. And thanks also to the ex-Peachpit team—you are missed.

Jocelyn Howell (Rocky Nook): You are an absolute star and without you this book would have been a pile of non-coherent gibberish. Thank you for your patience and for keeping me on the straight and narrow from start to finish.

Paul Crow: Mates from minute one of day one, thick as thieves, my old "work wife," and a top mate!

Mike Sullivan: You were a huge influence on my life since back in the late eighties. You pushed me and encouraged me, and you even introduced me to my wife. We did marathons together! And look at us all now. Thank you, mate, from the heart of my bottom. And no Mike, you can't! Stop asking!

Lee & Jamie Sullivan: I knew you wouldn't let me down!

Rob & Sandie Edwards: The best of friends and a huge part of my life. Glad you are godparents to our daughters. We've shared so many awesome memories from trips away to TV recordings, cup final days, and Butlin's weekenders. Great parents, great people. Love ya!

Alex & Aaron Edwards: My two godchildren—blame your parents. ;)

Tony Harmer: The Design Ninja. What you don't know isn't worth knowing. You are such a great mate. I always enjoy every minute we spend together, talking or sometimes podcasting. It's been a real pleasure getting to know you more over the past few years. My fellow Vectorgenerian.

The KelbyOne Family, Past & Present: Corey Barker, Matt Kloskowski, RC Concepcion, Dave Cross, Pete Collins, Larry Becker, Brad Moore—going from watching you and learning from you to becoming friends, peers, and colleagues is beyond superlatives. Thank you for all you continue to give to this incredible industry. To ALL the staff at KelbyOne, past and present—you guys rock! Lynn, Kathy, Jeanne, Ron, Victor, Margie, Kim, Jess, Cindy, Juan, Christina, Jason, Diane, all of you—you are the best! My ex-producers Steve, Meredith, and Jen—you all always welcome me and make me feel at home at HQ and Photoshop World.

Nancy Masse: For opening the door to this adventure!

Kathy Waite: We all love you! Thank you for being our queen, our Adobe person, and for looking after us all.

Special Mention for Chris Main: *Photoshop User Magazine* is the best publication and I'm proud to be a contributor. It was the original reason I joined NAPP, and you do an incredible job sir! I'm proud to write for you.

Astute Graphics: Nick & Susan van der Walle: (and the Astute fam, Camilla, Lorna, Irina, Dan, Kim, and our team of engineering wizards) Best job ever! Thanks for having faith in me and letting me loose! Nick & Susan, you have brought greatness to the world of design I am proud to be part of that history!

Aaron Draplin & Leigh: You have been so influential in my recent design life. Sometimes it takes one person to open your eyes to a different world, and you did that for me. To become your friend and spend time with you is just brilliant, and you still keep working so hard and showing us how to enjoy and appreciate the best of design around us. Dodgy geezers! Field Notes and merch—the addiction! To our dads in the Cosmos! Your mum is awesome—hello, Lauren Draplin! Oliver, do your homework!

Pete Poulton: A creative genius, always ahead of the curve and a damn good bloke! Thank you, mate, you've been a big part of my journey!

Dustin Lee: Mate! So glad we became friends. I love your work ethic, your creative mind, your generosity, and most of all, your friendship. RetroSupply rocks!!

The Worldwide Adobe Evangelists, Russell Preston Brown & Julieanne Kost: You have been incredibly inspirational and your hard work is very much appreciated.

Joe McNally & Annie Cahill: Joe, I appreciate your kindness and friendship, a benchmark of how to be dedicated and hardworking with passion. Annie, you are a sweetheart and a very talented one at that! It's an honor to call you both friends.

Moose & the Peterson Family: A gentleman amongst gentlemen. I'm proud to teach alongside you at Photoshop World and be your friend. You have an awesome family.

My Fellow Photoshop World Instructors: There are too many to mention, but I am proud to have been on the same bill as you all. We can all say we performed in Vegas :)

The InDesign Community & InDesignSecrets: A great resource and community. Bart van de Wiele, Nigel French, David Blatner, Anne Marie Concepcion, Mike Rankin, Khara Plicanic, and everyone who teaches InDesign.

I am blessed with so many great friends and influences in my life. To name a few, in no particular order because I can, and apologies if I missed anyone—next book, I promise:

Thanks to Toby Martin (Extensis); Unit Editions; Sean Ferguson; Amy and Joel Grimes; Jesus Ramirez; Craig "Hawkings" Smith; Nick Sambrato and Mama's Sauce; Doc and Julie Reed; Paul Shipper; Matt Dawson; Nick Burch; Jon Bessant; Danny Lenihan and 3LT team; David McClelland; the Roussells; Rob Sylvan; Dickie Pelham; Bill and Michelle Bolton and family;

Melanie, Andy, and Lilith Peck; Keith Richards and Ronnie Wood; Jim Coudal and Bryan Bedell from Field Notes; Jonny Sullens, Ruth, Hazel, Rich, and the Future Team; Mark Brickey; Billy Baumann; DKNG; Sean Mort; Chris, Joan, and Lucy Maycock; Mark Devlin; HE Creative; Dinah Hillsdon; Franz Hoffman and Fontself; the Simpsons; Keokuk; Sebastian Bleak; Ian Sayers; Mark Heaps; Mat Hayward; Theresa Jackson; Bill Gardner; Daniel Gregory; Peter Treadway; Lisa Carney; Dave Williams; The Field Nuts; Diane Gibbs; Chris Fields; Kaylee and Sam; Tad and Jessica Carpenter; Amy and Jen Hood; Kim Brockie; Mike Jones; Creative South; Damian Kidd; Mark Hirons; RobZilla; Dan Mumford; Creative Rush—Studio Heat; Von and Savannah Glitschka; Dan Stiles; Lenny and Bella Terenzi; Ian Barnard; Brandon Heiss; Bob Ewing; Rocky Roark; Scott Fuller; Scotty Russell; Darold Pinnock; Brian White; Peter Deltondo; Tom and the DC team; Russell Purdy; Matt Pereira; the Professional Imaging family (The 3 Petes); Marc, Gemma, and all the Ashby crew; Rocco, Nick, and the team at MPD; Alex Lowe; Sam Delaney; Mike Leigh; Bam and Streetboy; The Master of One guys, Andrew, Patrick, and Luke; Jason Frostholm; Dean Hazell; the FFIT guys; Stephen and David Wildish; Dave Thomas AKUTRs; The Dirty Strangers (past and present); the East Paddock chaps; all my Excalibur friends; Joanne Ayres; Matthew Weare; Lee Hodges; Queens Park Rangers—my team.

***He Shoots, He Draws* Podcast Listeners & Guests:** Thank you for all your support. Leave reviews on iTunes, please!

Photo Credits: Thank you Glyn Dewis, Alan Hess, Dickie Pelham, Aaron Blaise, Julian Calverley, Dustin Lee, Michael Poehlman, Aaron Draplin, Adobe Stock, and Scott Cowlin. (See below for specific image credits.)

All images by Dave Clayton, except the following: Glyn Dewis–19, 39, 44, 50, 62, 77, 79, 80, 82, 84, 118, 120, 173, 174, 175, 176, 177, 178, 181, 186, 242, 260; Aaron Blaise–19, 50; Alan Hess–26, 106, 162, 179, 180, 181, 184, 187, 191, 192, 195, 205; Julian Calverley–77, 79; Retro Supply, Dustin Lee–119; Dickie Pelham–185, 224; Michael Poehlman–251; Aaron Draplin–251; facundito (Adobe Stock)–cover, xxii, 42, 60; 9parusnikov (Adobe Stock)–60; Andrey Kiselev (Adobe Stock)–168, 181, 182; mrcats (Adobe Stock)–193.

About the Author

Dave Clayton is a UK-based graphic designer and creative specialist with over 30 years of design and marketing experience. With a great passion for all things design, Dave loves working in InDesign, Photoshop, and Illustrator. He specializes in creating branding projects and logos and has had design work published by many outlets, including Rocky Nook and KelbyOne.

Dave is also a KelbyOne and Photoshop World Instructor and writes for *Photoshop User* magazine. He is the co-host of the popular photography and design podcast, "He Shoots He Draws" with fellow Rocky Nook author Glyn Dewis. Dave is an Adobe Influencer and can often be found at design conferences learning, networking, and teaching. For more information on Dave, visit his website at www.itsdaveclayton.com and connect with him on social media @itsdaveclayton.

Table of Contents

Table of Contents

Chapter 3   51
How to Work with Frames and Objects
Getting Your Content Where It Needs to Be

Table of Contents

Chapter 4   83
How to Work with Text and Type
It's What InDesign Was Made For!

Table of Contents

Chapter 5   121
How to Work with Styles
Saving Time Stylishly

Chapter 6   137
How to Work with Color
Swatches, Gradients, Tints, and More!

Table of Contents

Chapter 7   169
How to Work with Images and Graphics
Become a Graphics Master

Table of Contents

Chapter 8   197
How to Customize Tables
Make Your Data Look Professional

Table of Contents

Table of Contents

Chapter 11   261
Plug-ins, Scripts, and Other Cool Stuff
Adding More to Your Toolbox

Foreword by Scott Kelby

As Editor for the *How Do I Do That?* book series, I cannot tell you how honored and excited I am to introduce you to this book, and in particular its author, Dave Clayton. When the publisher of this series talked with me about extending the concept to include other creative applications, I had my choice of hundreds of talented authors and educators throughout our industry, but my handpicked choice to launch the expansion of this series was Dave.

I knew Dave would be the perfect choice to author this book for three reasons: First, Dave is all about design and graphics. He loves it; he lives it. He's made his living as a professional graphic designer as long as I've known him, so he's not just someone who talks the talk—he lives it. He's got ink on his hands and a Wacom stylus in his shirt pocket and his passion for design, and for helping others learn it, comes through in every thing he does.

Second, Dave is a great communicator, a gifted educator, and someone for whom teaching is truly a calling. He gets so much joy by seeing others succeed and grow in their design skills and he is constantly sharing his knowledge of the Adobe Creative Cloud applications in online courses, magazine articles, and blog posts, on social media, and at major educational conferences where he's become a much sought-after speaker.

And lastly, I wanted Dave to be the first outside author to pen a book in this series because not only is Dave an awesome writer and teacher, Dave is just one of the best people on this planet. Dave is that guy that you meet and five minutes into the conversation you feel like you've known him your whole life. When you mention Dave's name in any group of creative professionals, you can count the seconds before someone in the group says, "Don't you just love that guy?" The mention of his name brings smiles and accolades from his peers, and I cannot tell you how genuinely thrilled I am that Dave is the author of *How Do I Do That In InDesign?* I know you're going to love him, and love learning from him too.

InDesign is a very special program for me. Its predecessor, Aldus PageMaker (later purchased by Adobe) was the first design program I ever used, and when Adobe launched its big brother Adobe InDesign some years later, I was one of the first to jump onboard. All these years later, I still use InDesign nearly every day in my own work (I've been using it today), and it's such an elegant, well-crafted, joy of a program to use, with so much hidden flexibility "under the hood." I'm just tickled that Dave will be the one to help you uncover its real power and learn how to work smarter, faster, and get more work done in InDesign in less time than ever.

I'll never forget being at the Photoshop World conference and sitting in on one of Dave's sessions. I believe it was called "InDesign Tips and Tricks," and although I figured I would know all the tips, I wanted to sit in on the session just because I could listen to Dave talk about literally anything. Heck, he could do a talk on how milk is pasteurized, and he'd find a way to make it interesting and entertaining. Anyway, he started the class with a really cool type tip (one I absolutely did not know) and son-of-a-gun, all these years of using InDesign and the very first tip blew me away, and changed the way I work in InDesign from that day on. In reality, he's already forgotten more about InDesign than I'll ever know, and that's exactly the type of InDesign expert you want to be learning from.

What Dave has done with this book is put the answers you need about InDesign right at your fingertips. If you're stuck with how to do something, just turn to that page, and Dave tells you right there—short, sweet, and to the point—exactly how to do it. You'll love Dave's writing style, and you'll truly appreciate his ability to take features and concepts that should be hard and make them so easy and understandable that you're immediately able to add them to your InDesign workflow. I'm so proud of what Dave has done with this book, but if there's anything in this book that I'm going to take credit for, it's that I know 100% I picked the right man for the job.

Have fun and enjoy the ride!

Cheers,

Scott Kelby
How Do I Do That? Series Editor

Photo © Erik Valind

Introduction

This is my first book with Rocky Nook. In fact, it's my first book ever. So I need to make this introduction count. If you don't believe me, check out my acknowledgments—I am milking this moment!

Many moons ago I found my first experience in computer design to be in desktop publishing, back in the day when it was still called that. I began my computer-aided design with Quark Xpress; you remember them? Anyway, DTP, as it was abbreviated back then, enabled me to make forms, small booklets, and stationery. Given that I used to use paper, scissors, and glue, it was a futuristic technological advancement to do this on a computer.

Time passed and I flirted with a few DTP software programs along the way—some were flings, others were longer-standing relationships—but once InDesign came along, my head was turned and my heart was stolen. This sounds dramatic, but this is my book and I said I was going to milk it!

InDesign came into our lives in 1999 and was the first real Mac OS–native DTP application. It took a couple of years before it was included as part of the Adobe Creative Suite. I was already a Photoshop and Illustrator user; hell, I even dabbled with Dreamweaver, but we all have our experimental phase when we are young!

I was hooked and InDesign became my favorite app to use, as I preferred designing brochures, flyers, and anything else that was needed in a marketing or corporate environment. That's where I spent most of my working years. I learned from so many people, including Scott Kelby, Terry White, David Blatner, Anne-Marie Concepcion, and the ever-growing InDesign community. I went on to take my InDesign ACA with a UK-based Adobe training center called Certitec, where I learned so much more from Jon Bessant, my instructor.

I was a member of the National Association of Photoshop Professionals (NAPP), founded by Scott Kelby and based in Oldsmar, Florida. NAPP became KelbyOne, and I had a great conversation with Scott about there being more InDesign content available for anyone who was looking to make a start in InDesign and who was confident to click on that little Id icon in their menu bar. From this chat I was asked to teach video classes on InDesign, which then led to a regular InDesign magazine article published in *Photoshop User* magazine for a year, and then to teaching about InDesign at Photoshop World four times (2016–2019), alongside the very people from whom I had learned so much.

My enthusiasm for InDesign comes from enjoying the product and what you can make with it. The great thing about this software is that just when you think you know all you need to know, boom, a new tip or trick comes along and you wonder why you ever spent so much time going the long way around. I am not an expert, I don't know every single thing it does—that's the joy of using and learning a creative tool—but I do love sharing and evangelizing InDesign to anyone who has yet to use it.

That's where this book comes from. Scott had written *How Do I Do That In…Photoshop*, *…Lightroom*, and *…Lightroom Classic*, three great titles from Rocky Nook. I nagged everyone that I would love for the series to be expanded and to have a similar style "recipe" book for InDesign. I was persistent. Very. But the outcome was less expected: Scott recommended I write it! Scott Cowlin and Ted Waitt agreed and for that I thank them! After the initial "Aaaaaaaaaargh," I calmed down and thought "why not?" So armed with a brief and knowing the kind of book I wanted, I set about listing all the tips and tricks I wish I had known when I first started using InDesign.

This book is not the InDesign bible, it's not comprehensive, it doesn't cover every single thing in InDesign. It's not meant to. Because if it did there wouldn't be room for me to write the updated version…kidding! Or am I? Anyway, it's a collection of tips and "how to" explanations to get you on the path to feeling comfortable using InDesign. I hope it helps you develop your path to becoming a more regular and better-equipped user of InDesign, and that you fall in love with the app. Not proper love—that would be silly—but close. ;)

Before You Start This Book

As I said in the first part of the intro (you read that, right?), this is not a fully comprehensive book of every single function and sub-function and sub-sub-function of InDesign. There's already a great InDesign book in the Rocky Nook collection that is more comprehensive, called *Adobe InDesign CC: A Complete Course and Compendium of Features* (Rocky Nook, 2019).

This book isn't that book! But I hope you are reading this because you purchased this book and that book. I want you to get the most out of this book by way of finding useful tips quickly. Think of it as a type of recipe book. "I want to make a Victoria Sponge to have with a nice cup of tea"—get out your recipe book, and there's a single page telling you how to make a quick Victoria Sponge accompanied by a lovely photo of said sponge. You could also get a bigger book with a very convoluted recipe and double the ingredients. My book is to help you get to your delicious sponge much quicker. I am very hungry now and the kettle is on. I digress.

As per Scott's previous books in this series, I have written this book as though I am sitting next to you, helping you find your way around. I am not getting too technical; I just explain where to find that tool or function and how to quickly apply it. Once we've got you there, you can further explore the settings and learn more about that function, setting, or technique. Once it's in your mind, you've got it, but if you forget, you know where to come back to!

I have included screenshots to help you along the way. I want to thank all of my friends who contributed images to this book (see page vii for photo credits). Yes, there are photos of me, my mates, and my kids—you know you would include them too if it were your first-ever book. ;)

How This Book Works

This book is broken into chapters to help you get to the right category of tips (e.g., type tips, image tips, color tips, etc.). It's not meant to be read in any kind of order. Just ask yourself "How do I…?" and head to the table of contents or the index to find the tool or tip name, and then go and read the info I have provided. Yes, there may be another way of doing it; that's fine. I'm showing you the way I use or the first method I think of when asked about a particular function or technique.

It's possible you'll only pick up this book for five minutes, get to the technique, and then put it down again. I would love for you to use it lots, wear it out, and then buy a new one. If nothing else, it'll help me pay to take my kids to Disney in a couple of years! But seriously, I want this book to assist you and become the buddy you'd normally call or text to ask, "how do I do this thing?"

If you haven't met me, I try my best to be helpful and nice to be around. Not everyone will like my style of writing or the way I explain things, but it was the only way I could write this book. If there's anything I have missed, and I'm sure there is, please write that tip down and share it with an InDesign-using friend or write it in the back of this book; there's a blank page after the index.

If you read these last three pages, thank you. If I still sent Christmas cards, you'd be on my list! If you REALLY enjoy using this book, please leave a review on Amazon to help others. Obviously, I would love to see good reviews, and if I get a chance to update this title in two or three years, I will be sure to take in all feedback and suggestions. Unless they are rude, of course. Just remember, my mum will be reading them. My mum is lovely—don't be mean and upset her. Now, she makes a lovely Victoria Sponge! And bread pudding! But she's rubbish at InDesign. Sorry, Mum.

Thanks to Tony Harmer for his help with the InDesign fun facts.

Chapter 1

How to Get Started

Getting Around InDesign Like a Pro

If you already use Photoshop or Illustrator, and it's highly likely you've experienced either or both, then you won't find the InDesign workspace too scary. If you haven't, run away now…kidding. One of the biggest obstacles when starting up a new application is that first time you see the workspace and it looks like one of those huge chalkboards full of important equations, including lots of strange icons, menus, panels, and terminology. It's okay, though, I am here to help. No need to hyperventilate and quit the program out of sheer panic. The first time I opened Photoshop, you could hear the gulp from 100 miles away. I scuttled straight back to Paint Shop Pro. But with the discovery of the National Association of Photoshop Professionals (NAPP), I fired that bad boy up again and worked my way around. It turned out Photoshop wasn't so mean to me and I actually understood what a lot of the menus were for and recognized what the tool icons were. Before long I had forgotten about poor old Paint Shop Pro and Adobe had me at "hello." Well, technically at File > New, but you get what I mean. So let's do the same with the InDesign interface. Throughout this chapter we'll go through what the workspace is showing you and I'll explain the various panels and menus. We'll cover how to set things up and get your defaults sorted—lots of tips and tricks to get you familiar with your surroundings. Before you know it, you'll be strutting around like the Fonz in Arnold's Drive-In. I always did wonder why a grown man used the Gent's bathroom as an office hangout, but if anyone could, the Fonz could! One cool thing to remember when you're working with any of the Adobe apps, and InDesign is no exception, is that you always have the Help menu if you need it. This is so useful for finding certain commands and menu items. It'll be your new best friend!

InDesign Fun Fact #1
Adobe first demonstrated InDesign (code-named K2) in 1998.

How Do I... Show or Hide the Control Panel?

With the introduction of the new Properties panel in InDesign CC 2019, you may find that the old-style controls are missing from the top bar below the menu functions. To get these back, just go to **Window > Control**, and the Control panel will reappear for all the tool functions that have controllable units. Once you get used to the new Properties panel you can switch the Control panel off by unchecking Control via the same method. This does free up a little real estate if that matters to you.

How Do I... Customize the InDesign Preferences?

Press **Command-K (PC: Ctrl-K)** to bring up the Preferences dialog. You can also access it by going to **InDesign (PC: Edit) > Preferences > General**. There are other options listed in the menu, but I suggest starting with General. You can access all the other options on the left side of the dialog that opens. The ability to view and change preferences is one of the most powerful features of any of the Adobe apps. That's exactly what they are, your preferences. We all like to work in different ways and this panel is where to get started.

How Do I... Change the Color of the Interface?

Open the Preferences dialog **(Command-K [PC: Ctrl-K])** and click on Interface in the column on the left. At the top of the dialog you will be presented with four shades of gray (not 50 shades!), ranging from dark to light. Click on one to choose the interface Color Theme. There is also a checkbox that gives you the option to have the pasteboard match the interface theme color. Sadly, you can't choose any other colors, but that might be a good thing!

How Do I... Enable or Disable the "Start" Workspace?

This is also in the Preferences dialog. Just go to **InDesign (PC: Edit) > Preferences > General**, and the option to Show "Start" Workspace When No Documents Are Open is right there at the top—check or uncheck as you wish. Just in case you aren't sure what this actually is, let me offer a quick explanation. When you open up InDesign without a document open, you'll get a start screen showing files you've recently opened, giving you a quick shortcut to open them again. With Show "Start" Workspace switched off, you'll just see the standard InDesign workspace, and you can go ahead and fire up a new document or go to **File > Open** to open the document you wish to continue working on.

How Do I... Go Back to Using the Legacy "New Document" Dialog?

Open up the Preferences dialog **(Command-K [PC: Ctrl-K])** and make sure you're in the General section. The second checkbox down is Use Legacy "New Document" Dialog. Add or remove a check mark to select your preferred method for opening documents. Do you notice the pattern emerging here? If you want to turn things on and off, always go to the Preferences dialog first.

How Do I... Open, Dock, and Collapse Panels?

To open any panel go to the Window menu and select the panel or panels you want to have in your workspace. Any panels that have a check mark next to them are already open. As you begin to open more panels, you can dock them together and dock them to the workspace. To dock panels together, click-and-hold on the top bar of one panel and drag it to the bottom or top of another. You will see a blue line appear where the panels will be attached. You can also dock the panels into the same group by dragging one panel on top of another, creating tabs for each panel. You can then access each panel by clicking on its tab. Once you've docked your panels to one another, click-and-hold on the very top of the topmost panel and drag it slowly toward the right or left of the workspace. When you see a long, vertical blue highlight appear along its edge, release your mouse to dock the panels to the workspace. Now if you resize the workspace, the panels will move with the frame. To collapse any panel in a group or on its own, just double-click its tab. You can resize any panel by dragging its edges or corners inward or outward. We'll cover how to save your new setup on the next page.

How Do I... Save, Delete, or Reset a Workspace?

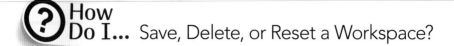

When you have your InDesign workspace laid out to your liking, you can save the setup by going to **Window > Workspace > New Workspace**. In the dialog that appears, give your custom workspace a name and use the checkboxes to save the Panel Locations and/or Menu Customization. Once you click OK, you can select this saved workspace, or one of the default workspaces, from the menu near the top-right corner of the interface. The default workspaces include: Advanced, Book, Digital Publishing, Essentials, Essentials Classic, Interactive for PDF, Printing and Proofing, and Typography. You can delete a custom workspace by selecting **Window >Workspace > Delete Workspace**. If you alter any of the default workspaces, you can reset them by going to **Window >Workspace > Reset [current selected workspace]**.

How Do I... Turn Tool Hints On and Off?

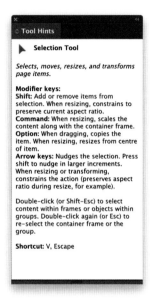

If you are still finding your way around InDesign, it might be a good idea to have Tool Hints switched on. To open (or close) the Tool Hints panel, go to **Window > Utilities > Tool Hints**. There is a hint for each of the tools in the Toolbar—the hint for the currently selected tool will be displayed in the Tool Hints panel. Once you become familiar with the tools you can turn this feature off. However, even when you think you know everything about a tool, you may be surprised every once in a while when you discover another action it can perform.

How Do I... Arrange My Open Documents?

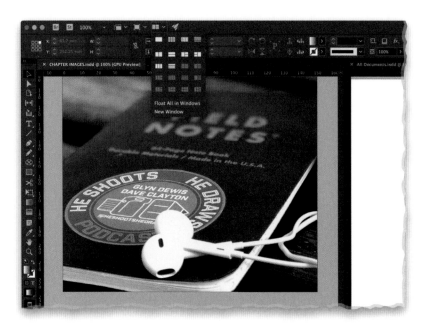

At the top of the interface where you see the Br and St icons (for Bridge and Stock), you'll see four more icons. The third icon is the Arrange Documents function, which gives you 20 options to help you lay out all your open documents. This is a great way to see all open files in your workspace if you are working on multiple documents. You can also go to **Window > Arrange**, but this menu offers fewer choices for layouts. If you want to go back to tabbed windows, then click on the first shape in the Arrange Documents pop-up menu, and this places all documents back into separate tabbed windows. You can also go to **Window > Arrange > Consolidate All Windows**.

How Do I... Hide the Desktop Screen Behind My Document?

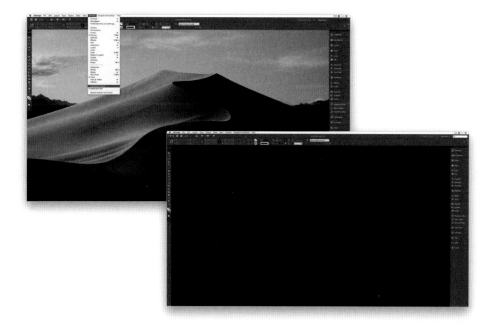

If you're using a Mac, when you first open an Adobe app, you can sometimes see your desktop in the back of the application. If you prefer to only see the actual application canvas, go to **Window > Application Frame** and make sure that option is checked. (*Note:* You won't see this option under the Window menu on a PC because Application Frame is the default.) I find it quite distracting to see my desktop screen behind the documents I'm working on, so I prefer to work with the Application Frame turned on. This will also reflect the theme color you have chosen as your workspace background. Once the frame is chosen, you can then resize the entire InDesign workspace by clicking-and-dragging the frame from any corner or frame edge.

How Do I... Find, Move, and Rearrange the Toolbar?

The Toolbar usually appears docked to the left side of the workspace. If you don't see it in your workspace, go to **Window > Tools** to open it. You can undock the Toolbar by grabbing the top and dragging it away from the edge of the frame. You now have a floating Toolbar. If you click on the little double arrows (>>) at the top of it, you can make it horizontal. When you have a horizontal Toolbar and click on the downward-pointing arrows on the left side, it changes into a two-column vertical Toolbar. Click on the double arrows (<<) again to change it back to one column. To redock the Toolbar, just click-and-drag the top of the panel over to the left or right side of the frame, and you'll see the vertical blue highlight appear when it is ready to dock.

How Do I... Show or Hide Rulers and Change Measurement Units?

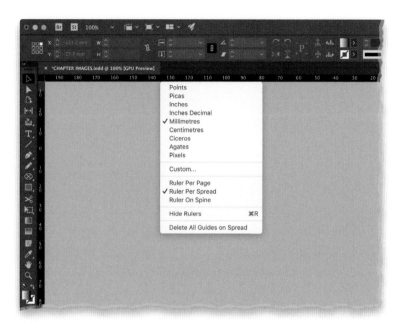

To toggle the rulers on and off, use the keyboard shortcut **Command-R (PC: Ctrl-R)**, or go under the View menu and select **Show Rulers** or **Hide Rulers** (the option changes depending on whether the rulers are currently visible). This will reveal and hide them at the top and left side of your document. When the rulers are visible, they will take on the attributes of the original document. So if you set the document in inches, then the ruler will be in inches. To change the unit of measurement, Right-click on one of the rulers and you will be presented with a pop-up menu giving you the following options: Points, Picas, Inches, Inches Decimal, Millimeters, Centimeters, Ciceros, Agates, and Pixels. You can change between these options at any time. The zero always defaults to the top-left corner where the rulers intersect. If you want your zero to start anywhere else in the document, just click in the small square where the rulers intersect and drag the zero to the new position. In the pop-up menu that appears when you Right-click on a ruler you can also choose to have them set to Ruler Per Page, Ruler Per Spread, or Ruler On Spine.

How Do I... Drag Out Ruler Guides?

When laying out a document you can drag out guides from the horizontal (top) and vertical (left side) rulers at the edges of the document window (these are the only places the rulers will be visible). Just click-and-hold on a ruler and drag your cursor to the desired location, then release your mouse to place the guide. To apply a guide to the entire spread, press-and-hold the Command (PC: Ctrl) key while dragging a horizontal guide. Pressing Option (PC: Alt) while dragging a guide from the horizontal ruler changes it to a vertical guide, and vice versa. If you want to abandon the guide before releasing your mouse, just hit the **Esc key**.

How Do I... Alter My Guides?

Press **Command-Option-G (PC: Ctrl-Alt-G)** to select all the guides on a page or spread. If you want to draw both a horizontal and a vertical guide at the same time, press-and-hold the **Command (PC: Ctrl) key** as you click-and-drag from where the rulers intersect at the top left of the document window (if the rulers aren't visible, press **Command-R [PC: Ctrl-R]** to toggle them on). If you're dragging out a vertical guide but want to quickly change it to a horizontal guide (or vice versa), press-and-hold the **Option (PC: Alt) key** as you drag. If you want to delete all the guides, Right-click on either ruler and choose **Delete All Guides on Spread**. You can also use the Smart Guides feature built into InDesign, which will give you visible guides that items will snap to when you're lining things up. To turn these guides on and off, just go to **View > Grids & Guides > Smart Guides**.

How Do I... Add a Grid to My Document?

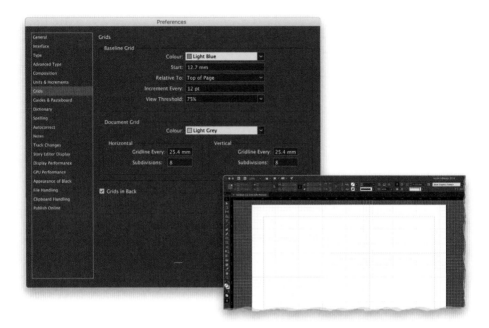

Sometimes you might prefer to work with a grid to help with precise placement of text and objects. Grids can be set up according to whatever preferences you choose. To do this, just go to Preferences **(Command-K [PC: Ctrl-K])** and click on Grids in the column on the left. Here, in the Document Grid section, you can adjust the grid color; the horizontal and vertical grid spacing and subdivisions; and whether the grid sits on top of the document—meaning it will be visible on top of anything placed in the document—or at the back of the document where it will be hidden underneath anything solid.

How Do I... Set Up Guides for Columns and Rows?

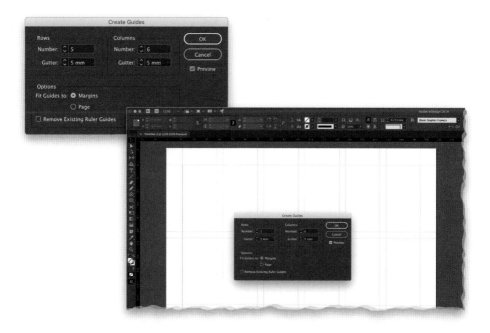

When setting up a new document, more often than not we use grids and guides to assist us with laying out objects on the page. It makes for a more structured and tidier layout. I prefer to set up my grid before placing any content. Let's take a look at how to do that with an example document. Create a new document **(File > New > Document)** with the following settings: Landscape orientation, A4 page size (297×210 mm), 6 columns, 5 mm gutters, 10 mm margins, and a 3 mm bleed all the way around. Click OK. Next, go to **Layout > Create Guides**. In the dialog that appears, tick the Preview checkbox so you can see what you're creating. Depending on your project, choose how many rows and columns you think you'll need. Because we created 6 columns when we created the document, we'll set the number of Columns to 6 and the number of Rows to 5 in this example. Before you click OK, look at the two choices for Fit Guides To: Margins or Page. Choosing Margins ensures that the guides line up with the margins; they don't line up if you choose Page. Because this is a document for print, we want to work within the margins and this is how the columns are set up. You can still place content up to the edges of the page, but make sure you allow for the page bleed with images.

How Do I... Check for Preflight Errors in My Document?

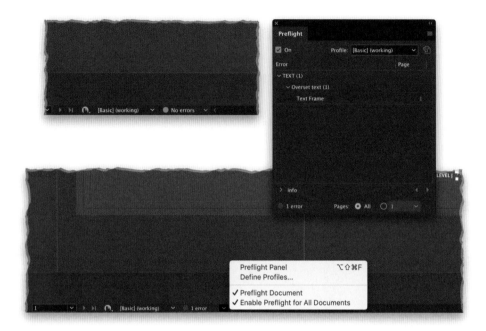

One of the biggest helpers in InDesign is the Preflight light. Where is this light? I'm glad you asked because once you know what its purpose is you will refer to it often while working in InDesign. The Preflight light is in the bar of icons at the bottom-left of the frame. When it's green, the world is good—your document has no errors and will export beautifully. If it's red it means, "Houston, we have a problem." Because you are placing images into your InDesign document and also laying out copy, every once in a while the source image might get moved or changed, or maybe the text box isn't large enough for your text—these are things that will affect your document's health. When you do see red and aren't sure what the problem is, just click the small down-facing arrow to the right of the light and choose **Preflight Panel**. This will open a panel that lists all the errors that need to be addressed in the document. When you double-click on an error, InDesign will jump to the section of your document where the error has occurred. In the example shown above, the text was overset, which means the text box wasn't large enough for the text. So we need to address that and, once we do, the light goes back to a healthy green.

? How Do I... Change to a Different Screen Mode?

Screen modes are really useful for seeing your print margins and jumping between layout mode and print mode. There are three ways to switch between screen modes. First, in the Application Bar (at the top of the window), click on the Screen Mode icon and you are presented with the following options: Normal, Preview (shown above, bottom left), Bleed, Slug, and Presentation (bottom right). The second way to select a new screen mode is to go to **View > Screen Mode**. Finally, you can press the **W key** on your keyboard to activate Presentation mode.

TIP: VIEW YOUR DOCUMENT FULL SCREEN
If you press **Shift-W**, Presentation mode takes you to full screen, hiding the InDesign frame and workspace. This is great for using InDesign as a presentation tool—just use the arrow keys to jump between pages or "slides."

How Do I... Zoom In and Out of a Document?

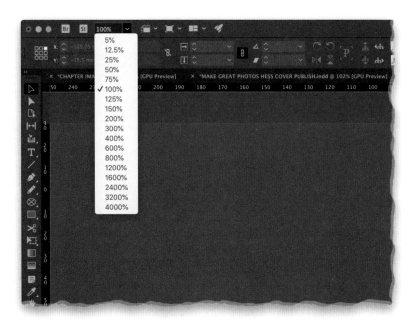

To zoom in and out of a document quickly, press **Command-+/– (PC: Ctrl-+/–)**. This is a default 25% increase or decrease zoom function. Pressing **Command-0** (zero; **PC: Ctrl-0)** will reset the document to show centered full screen. You can also go to **View > Zoom In** or **Zoom Out**. Another option is to use the Zoom Level pop-up menu in the top left of the frame. Just click on the down-facing arrow to the right of the current zoom level and choose one of the preset magnifications. InDesign will let you view your documents at any zoom level from 5% up to 4000%. When a document is open, its current magnification percentage will be displayed in both the Zoom Level field in the top Application Bar and next to the document filename in the document's tab (for example, MyDocument.indd @ 100%).

TIP: USE KEYBOARD SHORTCUTS TO CHANGE MAGNIFICATION
Here are some keyboard shortcuts to help you quickly change the magnification level of your document:

Command-2 (PC: Ctrl-2) for 200%
Command-4 (PC: Ctrl-4) for 400%
Command-5 (PC: Ctrl-5) for 50%

How Do I... Find Recently Opened Files?

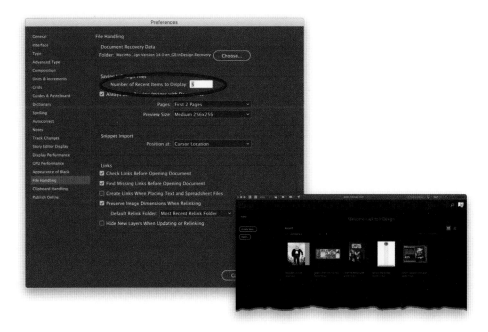

Aside from going to **File > Open** or pressing **Command-O (PC: Ctrl-O)** and then browsing for your files, you can also go to **File > Open Recent** and select a file from a list of previously opened documents. The beauty of this feature is that you can choose how many documents are displayed in that list. Open up your Preferences **(Command-K [PC: Ctrl-K])**, click on File Handling on the left, and in the field to the right of Number of Recent Items to Display, enter any number up to 30. I usually set mine to 10 or fewer (in the example above, I set it to 5) so that it's not too cluttered. The most recent document will always be at the top of the list. Another way to find your files is via the "Start" workspace, which must be enabled in your Preferences. Open your Preferences, click on General, and put a check mark in the box next to Show "Start" Workspace When No Documents Are Open. When you open InDesign, the "Start" workspace will show a number of your previously opened documents, based on the limit you chose in your File Handling preferences.

How Do I... Change the Pasteboard Size?

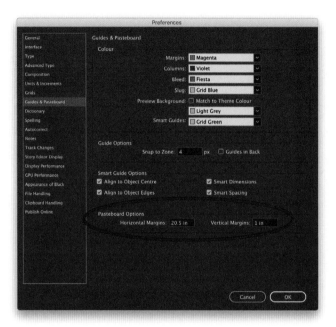

The InDesign pasteboard has smaller margins at the top and bottom than on the sides, but you can change this if you want. Maybe you have a lot of assets you want to place on the pasteboard while you work. To change the pasteboard dimensions, go to **InDesign (PC: Edit) > Preferences > Guides & Pasteboard**. Under Pasteboard Options near the bottom of the dialog, insert your desired Horizontal and Vertical Margins. You'll see the margins change when you click OK. This is all down to personal preference, but it's useful to know that you have some extra pasteboard space to use if you want it.

How Do I... Store My Assets?

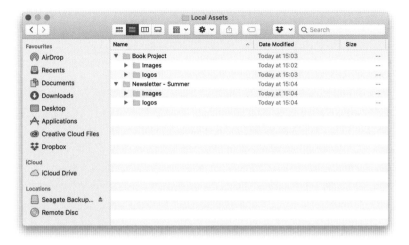

As a rule, I always gather all my assets and put them in a folder on my desktop. Why? Because if my Internet goes down and I have everything saved online, InDesign isn't going to like all of those broken links. Always create your folders and folder structure on your desktop as well as in your preferred cloud storage. When you've finished your project (or even as you're working), you can then save items in your CC Libraries or cloud storage as well. This also covers you if your computer develops any issues. Because InDesign relies so heavily on linked items, this workflow makes it easier to keep a healthy document and save or package elsewhere.

How Do I... Find, Add, or Change a Keyboard Shortcut?

If you find yourself using keyboard shortcuts, there's a quick way to check what shortcuts are assigned to what commands, and you can also change them or add new ones. To do this, go to **Edit > Keyboard Shortcuts**. A dialog will open where you can view and set all the shortcuts you desire. First, click on the Product Area pop-up menu (seen here top left) to select the type of commands for which you wish to view or apply shortcuts. In the Commands list below, you will see which commands are available for the selected product area. When you click on a command you will see the currently applied shortcut (if there is one) listed under Current Shortcuts. To edit or create a shortcut, select a command in the Commands list. Then click in the New Shortcut field at the bottom of the dialog, type the keystroke for your new shortcut, and click Assign. Click OK when you are finished.

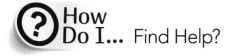

How Do I... Find Help?

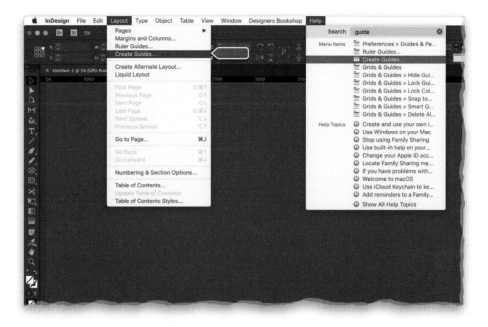

This is a final quick tip for when you're starting out. When you need a little extra help, InDesign is your friend. Looking for a command, but can't remember where it is? Then go under the Help menu, and begin typing your command into the Search field. InDesign will display a list of options (if available) and when you hover over an option, it will show you where that command is found in the relative menu!

Chapter 2

How to Work with Pages and Spreads

Setting Up Your Documents

For me, this is what InDesign is all about: making pages of documents with the most powerful tools available to the publishing world. InDesign is the tool for making anything from a single-page document to a mammoth book. Pages and spreads allow you to set up your document professionally and efficiently. In this chapter, we'll be looking at how to set up your first document, and will cover the range of settings available to you prior to beginning a project. We'll also look at how to set up your all-important master pages, and how to edit, rearrange, resize, and even color code them to make them easy to identify within a document. When you first start making documents, you can pretty much go with many of the default settings, but you have so many more options available to you. You can set up multi-use documents or very unique ones—the tools are all here. And we're not just talking print; InDesign is super powerful and versatile when it comes to making documents for the web. We aren't stuck with default print sizes; we can also use a multitude of web sizes and even device-specific sizes, such as those suited to an iPhone. In the 20 years that we've had InDesign, it has evolved to suit the ever-changing design landscape, and it continues to do so. Don't ever doubt what you can create in InDesign, and pages and spreads is where you're going to be creating your amazingly designed files.

InDesign Fun Fact #2

The first InDesign User Group was started in 2001 by Noha Edell.

How Do I... Create a New Blank Document?

This is a straightforward task, but there are some settings to consider (see next tip). Go to **File > New > Document** to bring up the dialog. Depending on how your Preferences are configured, you will see one of two dialogs: the legacy New Document dialog (above left) or the New Document dialog that resembles the "Start" workspace and shows Recent documents (above right). You can create your document by either choosing one of the predetermined sizes available in the dialog (if using the "Start" workspace) or creating a custom size. If you check the Preview checkbox at the bottom of either New Document dialog, you will see the new document behind the dialog. If this is just a one-off document, enter your preferred settings and go ahead and click Create. Once you've done this, you can then save the document.

How Do I... Set Up New Document Pages?

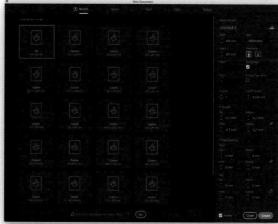

Most of the new document settings are self-explanatory, but there are a few I'd like to expand on. Both the legacy New Document dialog and the "Start" workspace offer the same options, but sometimes they're called something different, so I've distinguished them with the following labels, when necessary: (L) = Legacy; (N) = New.

Document Preset—If you've created a document preset you'd like to use (see pages 30 and 31), select it here.

(L) Intent / (N) Print/Web/Mobile Tabs (at top)—How do you intend to output the final product? The default option is Print, but Web and Mobile options are available.

Primary Text Frame—Honestly, this is for more complex documents with large amounts of flowing text. Leave this unchecked for now.

(L) Gutter / (N) Column Gutter—These are the gaps between columns (if you have columns). The gutter width should be set to a value that is at least equal to the point size of the text, but for most projects you can use whatever looks easiest on the eye.

Bleed and Slug—The bleed is the area beyond the edge of your document for printers to cut, the standard being .125"/ 3mm (some printers may require more for things like large banners). This ensures any edge-to-edge colors or images are trimmed to the very edge of the page. The slug (which I rarely use) is the area where you can include document info and notes.

How Do I... Create and Save Custom Document Presets (Using the "Start" Workspace)?

If you plan to use a specific document setup over and over again, it makes life easier to save that setup as a preset so you don't have to adjust all the settings every time. To create a preset, start by going to **File > New > Document**. On the right side of the New Document dialog, enter your document requirements. In the image above, I went for an A4 document (210mm × 297mm) with the following settings: Portrait Orientation, 6 Pages, Facing Pages, 6 Columns, 3mm Column Gutter, 10mm Margins, and 3mm Bleed. Once you've entered your settings, click on the little icon in the top-right corner of the dialog (circled above), next to where you add the document name. This allows you to save your settings as a Document Preset. Now give the Document Preset a name so it's easy to find again, and then click Save Preset. This particular document setup will now be available in your Saved items in the New Document dialog.

 Create and Save Custom Document Presets (Using the Legacy New Document Dialog)?

If you are creating a new document and have set your Preferences to Use Legacy "New Document" Dialog, then this would be a good time to create a new document preset. Go to **File > Document Presets > Define**, and you will be presented with the Document Presets dialog (above left), where you'll see a list of any existing presets. Click New to open the New Document Preset dialog (above center). Set your preferences and click OK, and you will be taken back to the Document Presets dialog, where you will see your new preset listed. You can edit any preset by highlighting it in the Presets list and clicking Edit. Once you've made your changes, click OK. Now when you create a new document, just go to **File > New Document**, open the Document Preset pop-up menu at the top of the New Document dialog, and you'll see your custom preset in the list (above right). Choose the one you want to use, and the associated settings will populate the dialog.

? How Do I... Switch Between Open Documents?

If you have multiple documents open in InDesign, it's easy to switch between them. There are a few ways to do so, but the quickest is to press **Command-`` ` `` (PC: Ctrl-`` ` ``)**. (The `` ` `` character is located on the same key as the ~ character.) You can also open the Window menu—where a list of currently open InDesign documents is displayed at the bottom—and select the one you wish to view. The document currently being viewed has a check mark next to its name. A third method is to click on the tab near the top of the workspace that contains the name of the document you wish to view.

How Do I... Find and Edit Master Pages?

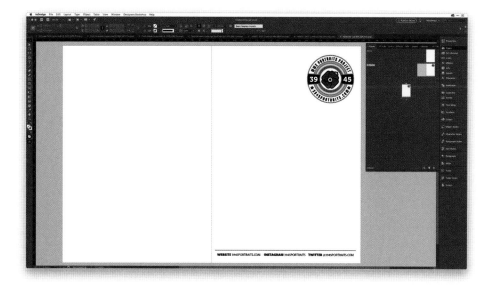

If you have a document open, its pages will show in the lower section of the Pages panel. (If you don't see the Pages panel, go to **Window > Pages** to open it.) The top section of the Pages panel shows the master pages. But what are master pages? Imagine you are working on a multi-page document, or even a single-page document, and you have fixed items on the page. You may accidentally click on one of these items and change or move it. You could lock the items down in the Layers panel to keep this from happening, but that's not the best way to handle it. This is where master pages come into play. A master page contains the consistent elements that are repeated on other pages, such as page numbers, a logo, an address at the bottom of the document, or even a website address or contact details. Treat a master page like a single document. To edit it, just double-click on the A-Master page icon in the Pages panel, and it will appear onscreen in the main document workspace, just like a regular document. This is the default master. You will have a left and right master. Now place any content—such as a logo and contact details—in the areas where you want it to repeat on each page. Once you are done, double-click on your document icon in the Pages panel (below the master page icons), and your master page is set. You can create more than one master page (the next would be B-Master, and so on), with different content on each one, to apply to your documents. We'll discuss how to apply a master page to a document in the next tip.

How Do I... Apply Master Pages to Document Pages?

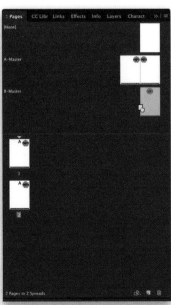

Once you have created all of your master pages, it's time to apply them to the pages in your document. By default, whichever master page you set first will be assigned to any new page you create. If you need to apply a different master page to any page in your document, there are a few ways to do so. One option is to go to the Pages panel and Right-click on the icon for the page to which you want to apply a different master, then select **Apply Master to Pages**. In the Apply Master dialog, select the appropriate master page and the page to which you want to apply it. You can also access this dialog by Right-clicking on a master page icon in the Pages panel. (*Note:* You can use this dialog to apply the selected master page to a single page or to All Pages.) Another option is to click-and-hold on the required master page icon in the Pages panel, and then drag it onto the appropriate document page icon below. For example, if you add a new page and it adopts the A-Master, but you want it to use to the B-Master, you can click-and-drag the B-Master page icon onto the newly added document page icon, and the elements on that page will change from the A-Master elements to the B-Master elements (notice the little hand icon dragging the B-Master downward in the image of the Pages panel shown above).

? How Do I... Add Additional Document Pages?

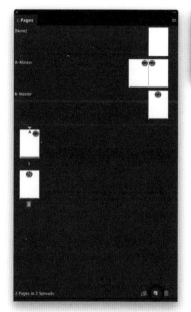

There are multiple ways to add additional pages to your document. The easiest method is to just click on the Create New Page icon at the bottom of the Pages panel. If you hold down the Command (PC: Ctrl) key when you do this, it adds a new blank master page instead. If you hold down the Option (PC: Alt) key when you click on the Create New Page icon, it brings up the Insert Pages dialog, where you can add multiple pages, choose where in the document to add the page(s) (After Page x, Before Page x, At Start of Document, or At End of Document), and decide which master pages should be applied to the new page(s). Make your selections, then click OK. The Insert Pages dialog can also be accessed by Right-clicking in the Pages panel and choosing **Insert Pages** from the context menu.

? How Do I... Rearrange and Delete Document Pages?

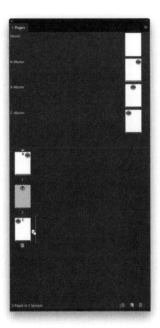

To delete a page from your document, just highlight its icon in the Pages panel and click on the trash can icon at the bottom of the panel. To move a page to a new location within the document, go to the Pages panel and click-and-drag that page's icon up or down to the location where you want it to appear. A line will appear indicating where the page will be located if released.

How Do I... Change the Size of Pages in a Document?

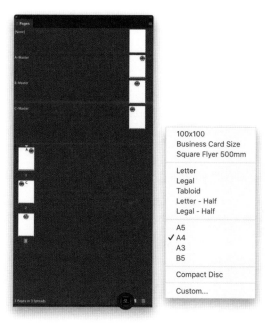

Go to the Pages panel and select the icon for the page you wish to resize, then click on the Edit Page Size icon (circled in the image above) at the bottom of the panel. You can choose from a list of predefined sizes or click on Custom and specify your own. You can also create different-sized pages in the same document. This is most useful if you are making multiple items in one document. Refer to the next tip for more information on how to do this.

How Do I... Use Different-Sized Pages in a Single Document?

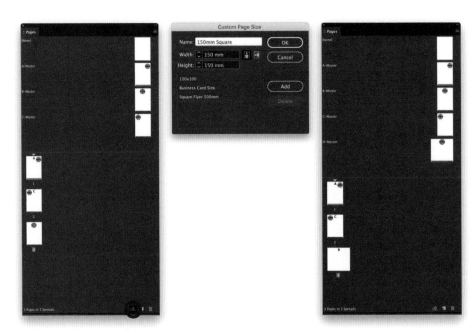

You can add additional pages to any document and resize them, maintaining all document settings (character styles, margins, bleeds, etc.) across the various pages Start by creating the first page as normal **(File > New > Document)**. Choose your settings in the New Document dialog, make sure you have Facing Pages unchecked, and click OK. Now open the Pages panel **(Window > Pages)** and click on the Create New Page icon at the bottom. Next, click on the Edit Page Size icon (circled above; to the left of the Create New Page icon) and choose a size. If you select Custom, you can create your own specific-sized pages, such as a business card, square flyer, or any size document you require. Repeat this action for each different-sized page you need to add to the document.

TIP: CREATE A NEW MASTER PAGE FOR EACH PAGE SIZE
When creating different-sized pages in a multi-page document you can't apply the standard master page to each new page because it is sized for the initial page size you created, but that's okay. Just click on each page icon in the Pages panel and drag it up to the master section to create a master size for that page size. You now have a master page set for that page size. Do this for each new page size you create. You may need to change the layout of the assets to suit the new page size. In the example above, the new size is a square, so the logo and text had to be repositioned. If you had already created your master first (some people do), then just create your new regular page and apply the master to it.

How Do I... Add Page Numbers to My Document?

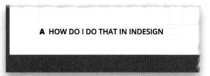

To set automatic page numbering in your document, you'll need to add a page number marker to a master page. When the master page is applied to your document pages, the page numbering will automatically be updated. (*Note:* When you set the page number on a master page, it is displayed as the master page prefix [e.g., "A"]. On the document pages, the correct page number will be displayed.) In the Pages panel, double-click on the master page to which you want to add your page number marker. Next, create a text frame on the master page that is large enough to hold the longest page number you expect to have, as well as any text you want to appear next to it. Position this text frame where you want the page number to appear on the page. For most publications, the page number is placed near the outer edge of each page. If your document has facing pages, you'll need to create separate text frames for the left and right master pages. In the page number text frame, add any text that you would like to appear before or after the page number, as per the example above. Position the cursor where you want the page number to appear, and then choose **Type > Insert Special Character > Markers > Current Page Number**. Finally, apply the master page to the document pages on which you want the page numbering to appear.

?How Do I... Make Sense of Pagination?

When you're designing a booklet, leaflet, or pamphlet for print, always remember to set out your pages in multiples of four. Think about it physically: get a piece of A4 paper and fold it in half. You now have four pages. If you add another sheet, it becomes eight pages—and so on, in multiples of four. This will make your local printer very happy! For a digital-only PDF, however, you don't have to think in terms of a booklet format. You can create as many or as few pages as you require. You'd be surprised how many people forget this!

? How Do I... Change the Layout from Facing Pages to Individual Pages?

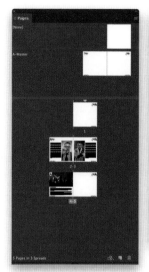

Sometimes you may want a document with individual pages, not with facing pages like you'd use for a booklet. This may be for a PDF or a series of different-sized pages in a single document, for example. It's easy to set this up. Go to **File > Document Setup** and uncheck the Facing Pages checkbox. This will rearrange your document into a series of individual pages. If you want to return to a book-style layout—with a single cover page followed by spreads determined by the number of pages in your document—simply put a check mark in the Facing Pages checkbox. The Facing Pages checkbox can also be accessed in the Properties panel when a page is selected.

? How Do I... Format a Page to Print to the Edge of the Paper?

When creating documents for print we often want certain images or areas or color to go to the very edge of the paper. To ensure that the color goes to the very edge of the paper when it is trimmed, you have to allow for bleed. Your local print company will advise you on the bleed amount they require. I often leave a 3mm bleed all the way around the document for small documents, and around a 5mm–6mm bleed for larger documents. You can set the bleed at the creation of the document, but in case you forgot to do so, just go to **File > Document Setup** and a dialog will open up—the same one you see when creating your document. Go to the Bleed and Slug section near the bottom of the dialog and add your required bleed. Make sure the link icon to the right of the Bleed fields is selected so that when you type a number into the first field and then click in another, all of the fields will change to the same bleed size. (*Note:* See page 254 for information on how to enable marks and bleeds for PDF export.)

TIP: ADJUSTING THE BLEED
A little tip I always credit to Jon Bessant, a great InDesign instructor, is to click in the first field and then continue to tap the up arrow key on your keyboard until you get to the required amount. All fields will increase at the same time. Too much? Just use the down arrow to decrease the amount.

How Do I... Save Time with Print Templates?

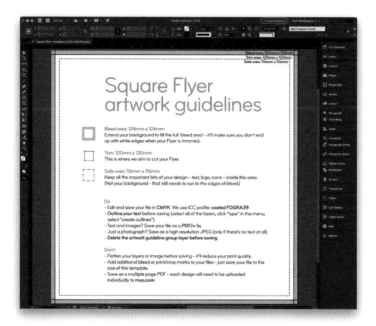

Many online print companies supply free templates for things like business cards, letterhead, and flyers, making it easy to set up your documents to their exact specifications. Ask your preferred online printer or local print company if they have templates of their own. MOO.com, for example, offers InDesign (IDML), Illustrator (PDF/AI), and Photoshop (PSD) templates (and sometimes a flat JPG graphic) to help you create your artwork for all of their products. Let's take a quick look at a how to find and use a template supplied by MOO (https://support.moo.com/hc/en-us/sections/200570950-MOO-Product-Templates). In the MOO Product Templates list, find the product you want to make (e.g., business card, flyer, postcard, etc.), and then look for the InDesign template download link. The template will be in IDML format because MOO doesn't know what version of InDesign you are using, and as explained elsewhere in this book (page 245), the IDML format is suitable for opening in many previous versions of InDesign. Click on the link to download your file, and then open it in your version of InDesign. You will immediately see that the template contains layers that display the bleed, trim, and safe areas in which to create your artwork, along with instructions on how to use the template and how to save your file for uploading. It's a good idea to download most of these templates for future use, as they are great for getting used to bleeds, trims, and safe areas for content. I suggest saving the IDML file as an InDesign Template File (.indt) for future use. You can also find cool templates on Adobe Stock (see page 273), or save your own custom documents as templates to use again later (see page 247).

How Do I... View a Completed Spread?

To view a completed spread and hide the bleed guides—and all other guides, in fact—just tap **W** on the keyboard. You will see the spread in Preview mode, as it would be printed. Tap the **Tab** key to hide all the panels as well, and tap Tab again to make them return. Press **Shift-W** to view the spread full-screen with no application frame. This is Presentation mode. Another way to hide all the guides is to go to **View > Screen Mode > Preview**. Select **Presentation** to view the spread full screen.

How Do I... Make Changes to My Document with the Properties Panel?

The new Properties panel in InDesign CC 2019 allows you to make document changes on the fly straight from the panel.

From the top down you can:

- Adjust the document size and orientation
- Manually change the width and height of the document globally
- Change the number of pages in the document and whether they are facing or not
- Adjust the top, bottom, and side margins
- Adjust the layout of the pages within the document (when you click on Adjust Layout, a new panel will open that allows you to change additional settings, such as the bleed value)
- Jump to a specific page in the document
- Disable or enable rulers, guides, and grids

How Do I... Move Content Between Documents?

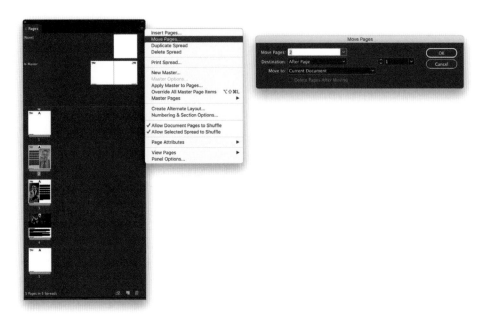

When you're working on two documents that are very similar and share some of the same content, there may be times when you need to move content from one document to the other. Copying and pasting is one option, of course, or you could duplicate or move an entire page or multiple pages. Start by going to the Pages panel and selecting the page(s) that you want to move. Then open the panel menu in the top-right corner of the Pages panel and choose **Move Pages** (or go to **Layout > Pages > Move Pages**). In the Move Pages dialog, you can select which page(s) you want to move and where you want to move them. Since you already had pages selected in the Pages panel, those page numbers will appear in the Move Pages field. The default option is to move the page(s) to another place in the same document, but you can choose any document that's currently open from the Move To pop-up menu. Once the document is selected, you can decide where in the new document you want the page(s) to appear. If you want the page(s) to be deleted from the source document after they are moved, put a check mark next to Delete Pages After Moving.

How Do I... Color-Code My Pages?

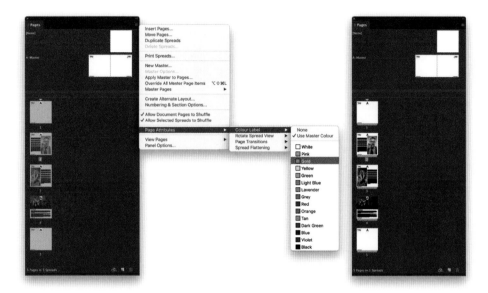

When you have a lot of pages in a document it's useful to color-code them. Start by selecting the pages to which you want to apply a color code in the Pages panel. To select a continuous series of pages, click on the first page you want to select, and then hold down the Shift key and click the last page in the series. This will select the first and last page and all pages in between. To select numerous nonconsecutive pages, hold down the Command (PC: Ctrl) key as you click on each page you want to select. Once you have selected the pages, click on the Pages panel menu, select **Page Attributes > Color Label**, and choose your color from the list. This will apply a color tab to each of the selected pages in the Pages panel.

How Do I... Make My Pages Panel Thumbnails Larger?

To make the thumbnails in your Pages panel a little easier to see (especially when you have a lot of pages), Right-click on a page or master page thumbnail and choose **Panel Options**. In the Panel Options dialog, set your Pages and Masters thumbnail sizes—Extra Small (for those of you with the vision of the Six Million Dollar Man), Small, Medium, Large, Extra Large, or of course, the biggest of them all, Jumbo! Pages and Masters can be independently resized; it's all about personal preference. In the Page Layout section at the bottom of the Panel Options dialog, you can also decide whether the masters or pages appear at the top of the Pages panel.

?How Do I... Find File Information About My Document?

To find information such as the current size of your document, all you need to do is check the Info panel (go to **Window > Info** [shortcut **F8**] if it is not already open). The document File Size is displayed at the bottom of the panel. The Info panel will also show you the location of the file, but you'll need to hover over this to see the full location because the panel cannot be resized. If you click on the panel menu and select **File Info**, you will be presented with another dialog where you can add more information about your document, such as Title, Author, Description, Copyright info, and other useful information that may be required. Be aware that if you click on an asset on the page, such as an image, the Info panel will display information for that element.

Chapter 3

How to Work with Frames and Objects

Getting Your Content Where It Needs to Be

Ever since InDesign came into our lives, the features I have always raved about, as simple as they are, are frames and objects. Both of these are shapes within which we place our content. Everything goes in a frame, and they are wonderful. They separate the men from the boys and the women from the girls when you compare programs like InDesign and Word (though it pains me to even compare these programs). Let's not talk about Publisher—is that even a thing anymore? Anyway, frames and objects are what make layout so much easier. Make a frame or an object, put your content in it, and place it where you want. It really is that simple. Even as far back as Quark, frames and objects is where the action is. Have I convinced you that they're awesome yet? You'll see in this chapter that with frames and objects comes great responsibility! You have so much control over how you create them, how they behave, what they can do, and how flexible they are for creating content. Whether it's text, images, tables, graphs, solid color—you name it—it goes in a frame. You can apply strokes to make your frames and objects stand out, and you can even create bespoke shapes with the Pen and Pencil Tools. You can place multiple frames and shapes into grids, apply fancy corner styles, and align them all beautifully. You can also set styles for them (but we'll talk about that in chapter 5). In this chapter, we'll walk through basic frame and object functionality, creativity, editing, and more. By the end of it, you'll be a frame and object master! That sounded much cooler in my head, but you get it. To paraphrase Aristotle, and because it makes me sound clever, "If you do something well at the beginning, you are halfway to a successful completion," so getting these tips and tricks in at the beginning of your workflow helps you get to a successful end result.

InDesign Fun Fact #3

The first edition of *InDesign Magazine* was published in August 2004.

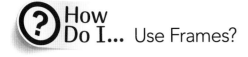

How Do I... Use Frames?

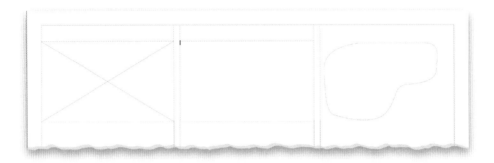

In InDesign, we place everything in some kind of frame, and each frame can be edited independently. That, for me, is why it is so much easier to create great-looking documents in InDesign than in an application like Microsoft Word. There are three kinds of frames: text frames, graphic frames, and unassigned frames. All frames and shapes can have strokes and fill colors applied to them. An unassigned frame is a shape that has been created manually, and by that I mean it can be created with a frame tool and reshaped with the Pen Tool **(P)**, or created with just the Pen Tool, and it doesn't always have to include text or graphics. All of these frames can be resized on the go and can be altered with the Direct Selection Tool **(A)** or the Pen Tool.

How Do I... Create a Frame?

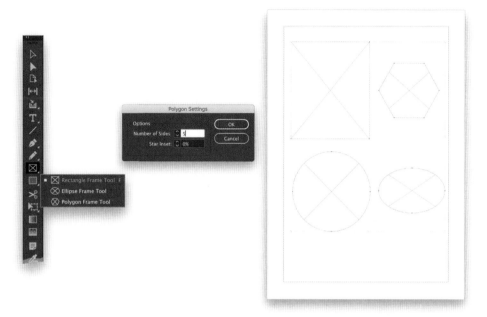

In the Toolbar, look for a rectangle (default) icon with an X in it—this is the Rectangle Frame Tool **(F)**. Click-and-hold on the icon to open the flyout menu, which contains three choices: Rectangle, Ellipse, and Polygon. To create a frame, simply select the frame shape you require, and then click on your document and drag out the frame. Press-and-hold the Shift key as you drag to keep the shape constrained. For example, holding the Shift key while dragging with the Ellipse Frame Tool creates a circle, and doing so with the Rectangle Frame Tool creates a square. By default, the Polygon Frame Tool will create a five-sided shape—a pentagon. But what if you don't want a pentagon? All you need to do is select the tool and click once anywhere in your document, and a dialog will appear for any of the frame options. The Polygon dialog allows you to decide how many sides you want the frame to have. Inputting a size won't matter too much at this point because you can resize the frame manually after you've placed it, but for precision you can go ahead and specify a size. To create a text frame, select the Type Tool **(T)** from the toolbar and drag out a shape for your text. This can be resized as needed after it's been created. When a text frame is selected, you can also go to **File > Place** and choose an image to place inside the frame. InDesign will convert the frame to a graphic frame and any text in the frame will be discarded and replaced with the image. You can also wrap text around a frame.

How Do I... Create a Shape?

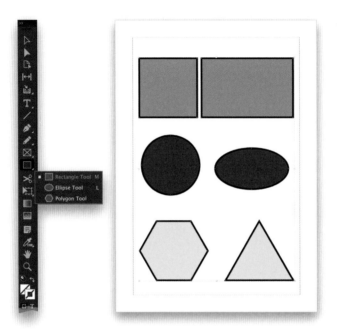

Shapes are like frames, but you can do a lot more with them. The shape tools (Rectangle, Ellipse, and Polygon) are found below the frame tools in the Toolbar and do not have an X within them. To create a shape in your document, Right-click on the shape tool in the Toolbar and select a shape from the flyout menu, then drag out a shape in your document. Hold the Shift key while dragging to constrain the proportions. You can also create a shape by simply selecting your shape tool and clicking once in your document. This will open a control dialog where you can determine the exact size of your shape. Click OK, and the shape will be added to your document. You won't see it yet because it will have no fill and no stroke; only the shape path will be in view once the shape is selected. Using the tips on strokes and fills (pages 55–57), you can give your shape some personality. Shape tools are usually used to create filled shapes, but these can easily be converted to accept text or an image. A shape is also known as an unassigned frame and can be created manually—with the Pen Tool **(P)**, for example. These are frames that aren't really meant to include any text or graphics, but they can if you need them to. You might draw shapes on your page for decoration; fill them with a background color; or if you are brave enough, you could even create a type of logo, just as if you were drawing in Adobe Illustrator. You can also wrap text around a shape.

How Do I... Apply a Stroke?

You can apply strokes, also know as line settings, to any paths, shapes, frames, and text outlines. When one of these items is selected, the stroke properties will be available to you. As with a lot of these tips, the Properties panel is a good place to start. The first thing to do to is give the stroke a color—without a color, a stroke won't be applied. Click on the little stroke icon (the square frame next to the word Stroke) in the Properties panel to open the color picker. Choose your color, and the stroke will be applied to your selected frame, object, or text. I chose red in the example above. Once you've selected a color, the default stroke thickness will be adjusted to 1pt, and this is your starting point.

How Do I... Change the Style of My Stroke?

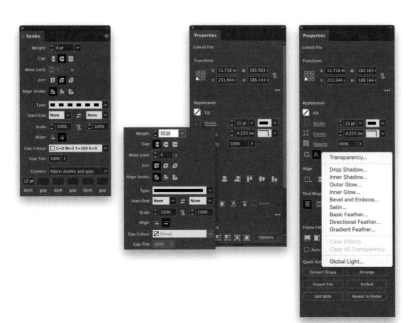

There are optional settings (in addition to weight and color) for all strokes, and these are found in the Stroke panel **(Window > Stroke)**. You can also click on the word Stroke in the Properties panel, and you will get a pop-up panel with all of the additional controls found in the Stroke panel, meaning you won't have to open up the Stroke panel at all. These stroke settings allow you to determine the thickness and line type; the type of corner or bevel shape; how the stroke segments join: the start and end shapes of the stroke (if there are open ends); the color between the gaps (if you choose a line type with gaps); and more—there are so many options! Within the Properties panel, you can even apply special effects to the stroke by selecting the ƒx icon below the stroke settings. But as the usual design rule goes, just because you can, doesn't mean you should—beware, there's a lot to get carried away with. But have fun exploring!

How Do I... Create Custom Strokes?

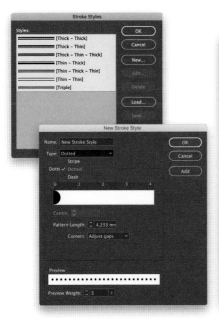

Want to build a custom stroke in InDesign? It's easy. Just go to the panel menu at the top-right corner of the Stroke panel **(Window > Stroke)** and choose **Stroke Styles**. A dialog will open with several options and a list of custom strokes. Click the New button to open the New Stroke Style editor. You can make dashed, dotted, or lined patterns; change the pattern length; and preview your designs at different weights. The custom strokes are saved on a document level, but you can save them and load them into other documents. To save a stroke, click on it in the Stroke Styles dialog, click the Save button, navigate to where you want to save it, and click OK. To Load a saved stroke, click the Load button in the Stroke Styles dialog, navigate to where you saved it, and click Open. If you want a custom stroke to be available as an option in all new documents by default, simply create the stroke with no document open.

How Do I... Insert Text in a Frame?

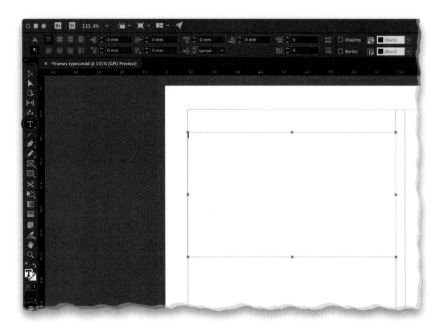

As mentioned previously, you can create a text frame by simply dragging one out with the Type Tool **(T)**. When you release your mouse, you'll see the cursor blinking in the upper-left corner of the frame, and you can just start typing. It's also really easy to add text to any other type of frame. Select the Type Tool **(T)** and click inside any shape to convert it into a text frame, and then, again, just start typing. (*Note:* This function can be disabled—see the next tip, "How Do I Turn Off the Auto Text Frame Feature?") You can also fill a frame with placeholder text to get a feel for what the document will look like when your copy is added. Simply insert your cursor into the text frame and go to **Type > Fill with Placeholder Text**. While a text frame is selected, you can go to **File > Place** and choose an image to place inside the frame, and any text in that frame will be discarded and replaced with the image. This is because InDesign has converted the frame to a graphic frame. To learn more about working with text in InDesign, head to chapter 4.

How Do I... Turn Off the Auto Text Frame Feature?

Not everyone wants the ability to automatically turn a frame into a text frame with the Type Tool **(T)**, especially if you have clumsy fingers and are prone to accidentally clicking in a frame with the Type Tool selected. This is a feature that can be switched off in Preferences. Just go to **Preferences > Type** and check or uncheck the box next to Type Tool Converts Frames to Text Frames (second option from the top).

How Do I... Replace Content in a Frame?

If you're replacing text, just copy your new text and paste it straight over the existing text. If it's an image you want to replace, the quickest way to do so is really simple: just select the frame, go to **File > Place**, and choose a new image. You'll notice that the Replace Selected Item checkbox at the bottom of the Place dialog is automatically selected. You can also drag and drop an image from a folder location into the selected frame. Use the Frame Fitting options to adjust the placement of your image (see pages 173 and 174). If you're copying an image, you can also use **Edit > Paste Into**, but pasting into InDesign documents is not recommended; placing is always the preferred method.

How Do I... Make My Frame Fit My Image?

Frame Fitting Options allow you to set your frames to fit the images they contain according to your needs. To access the Frame Fitting Options, either go to **Object > Fitting > Frame Fitting Options** or Right-click in the image frame itself and select the same menu options. This brings up a dialog where you can choose an automatic fitting option—None, Fit Content to Frame, Fit Content Proportionally, or Fill Frame Proportionally—from the Fitting pop-up menu, and select an alignment point. Finally, you can manually select the crop amount you may need around the image. For more on Frame Fitting Options, see pages 173 and 174 in chapter 7.

How Do I... Scale Frames and Their Content at the Same Time?

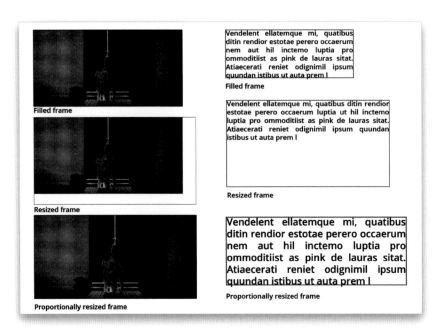

When you're scaling a frame that contains an image the behavior of the elements can be confusing at first. In the first example above, the frame fits the image (my two lovely daughters), but I want to make the frame larger to fill more of the page. If I just click-and-drag one corner of the frame to pull it out, the frame expands but the image does not. If I press-and-hold the Shift key while I drag, the frame resizes proportionally, but still without the image. To include the content of the frame as you resize it, press-and-hold **Command-Shift (PC: Ctrl-Shift)** as you drag, and everything will resize proportionally. This also applies to text—the text will resize in relation to the resizing of the frame. To make a text frame larger but maintain the original size of the text itself, just resize the frame as normal.

TIP: FITTING A FRAME TO ITS CONTENT

If you accidentally resize the frame and not the image, just double-click on one corner of the frame and it will snap to the image. Then you can continue to resize as you wish.

How Do I... Create Multiples of the Same Frame or Shape?

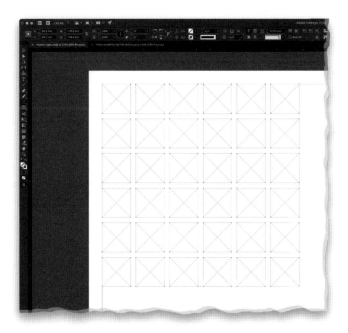

When you're creating a frame or shape, you can quickly and easily create multiples of it. As you're dragging out a frame or shape in your document, press the right arrow key to add copies of it horizontally (they'll look a little strange at first—we'll come to that in a moment). If you add too many, press the left arrow key to remove them. Now press the up arrow key to add a new line of identical shapes vertically, with the same quantity as the first horizontal line. Press the down arrow key to remove shapes. Do not release the mouse until you are happy with the quantity and layout of the shapes. If you want the shapes to be proportional, just press-and-hold the Shift key and release the mouse, and all of the shapes will appear in an equally aligned grid. You can do the same with images.

TIP: CREATING MULTIPLE POLYGONS

If you're working with polygons, start by setting the shape according to your needs. Select the Polygon Tool and click once on the document to open the Polygon dialog Enter the number of sides you need, then click OK. Once the shape is on the page, delete it. What you've just done is set the default for the Polygon Tool. Now when you drag out your shape, it will take the form of the last created polygon. Here's an even freakier tip: when you are dragging out a polygon and have already started to create multiples, without releasing the mouse, give the space bar a quick tap. Now the up and down arrows increase and decrease the number of sides on the polygon, and the left and right arrows adjust the inset values of a shape like a star.

How Do I... Create a Grid of an Existing Frame or Shape?

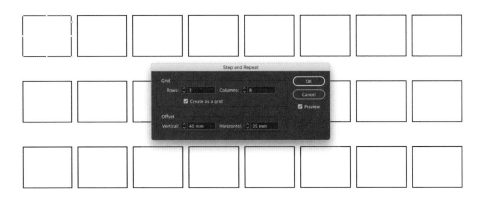

If you have already drawn out your frame or shape and you want to create a grid with multiples of that same frame or shape, first make sure it's selected, and then go to **Edit > Step and Repeat**. In the Step and Repeat dialog, put a check mark next to Create as a grid, as well as next to Preview so you can see what you are doing. Now simply enter the number of Rows and Columns you want in your grid. Use the Vertical Offset menu to increase or decrease the space between the rows, and the Horizontal Offset menu to adjust the space between the columns. Play with the settings and see what you get!

? How Do I... Modify the Shape of a Frame or Object (Part 1)?

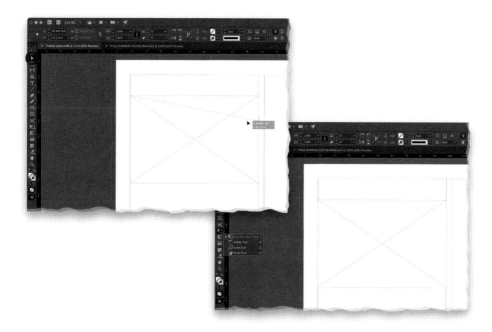

The first tool in your toolbox for quickly changing the shape of something manually is the Direct Selection Tool (**[A]**; solid arrowhead icon in the Toolbar). Simply choose it from the Toolbar and click on your frame. You can now click on any point on the frame and move it independently from the other points. When a point is selected, it will change from a small white point to a blue one. You can select more than one point at any time by pressing-and-holding the Shift key while you select your points. Use the arrow keys to move the points in small increments. You can also access other transform options from the Free Transform function in the Toolbar, including the following:

- Free Transform Tool **(E)**—Enables you to manually manipulate a shape
- Rotate Tool **(R)**—Enables you to rotate a shape from your chosen reference point
- Scale Tool **(S)**—Enables you to manually resize a shape from your chosen reference point
- Shear Tool **(O)**—Enables you to shear a shape from your chosen reference point

How Do I... Modify the Shape of a Frame or Object (Part 2)?

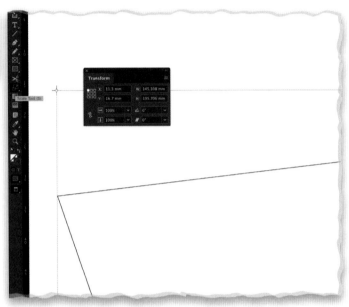

Go to **Window > Object & Layout > Transform** to open the Transform panel. You can use this panel to view and/or input more specific geometric information for a selected frame or shape, including values for position (X & Y coordinates), size (W & H percentage), rotation (by angle), and shearing (also by angle). You will also see what's called the Reference Point Grid (circled above left). This grid allows you to ensure that all transformations originate from a fixed point on or near the object. A crosshair-style icon is displayed at the reference point in the document when a transform tool (such as the Scale Tool **[S]**) is active to show you where the object will be scaled or altered from. There is also a constraining link available in the Transform panel if you wish to make your changes in a constrained manner.

How Do I... Change the Corners of My Shape?

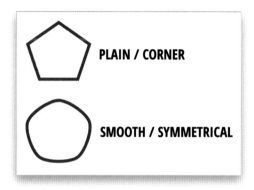

PLAIN / CORNER

SMOOTH / SYMMETRICAL

One quick way to transform a shape is to use the Convert Point options (also known as anchor points—if you use Illustrator you'll be familiar with anchor points) to change the corners of the shape. For example, if you want to make a corner of your polygon shape more rounded, select the point on that corner and go to **Object > Convert Point > Smooth** (or Symmetrical). This is just a quick tip, but it could be useful sometimes, especially when you want a shape that is more rounded than the standard shapes and you want to convert it quickly. If you are familiar with the PenTool **(P)**, you'll find that having Smooth and Corner points makes a difference in how you would change the shape with the PenTool.

How Do I... Create a Rectangle with Rounded Corners?

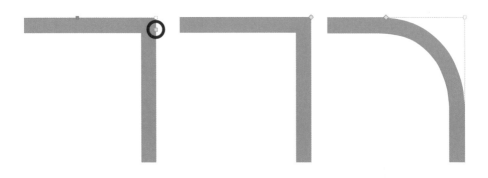

When you draw out a square or rectangle shape, sometimes it's nice to have rounded corners. The control used to create rounded corners is one of those that is right there in front of you, but unless someone shows it to you, you don't realize it's there. We've used it in a previous tip for corner options, but here I'll show you how to use it to make nice rounded corners, and how to use it on independent corners as well. First draw out your shape, and then choose the Selection Tool **(V)** from the Toolbar. You'll see a little yellow square appear on the right side of the frame, near the top-right corner. Click once on the yellow square, and it will turn into a diamond and jump to the corner of the frame. You'll also see yellow diamonds appear on the other three corners of the frame. Now you can drag any of those yellow diamonds left or right to increase or decrease the roundness of the corners. If you press-and-hold the Option (PC: Alt) key and click on any of the corner diamonds, you can change the corner style by rotating through the available options one by one. You can then drag the yellow diamond in or out to adjust the effect. To alter only one corner at a time, press-and-hold the Shift key as you drag the diamond for that corner in or out. Press-and-hold **Option-Shift (PC: Alt-Shift)** and click on a corner to change the style of only that corner.

How Do I... Apply Corner Styles?

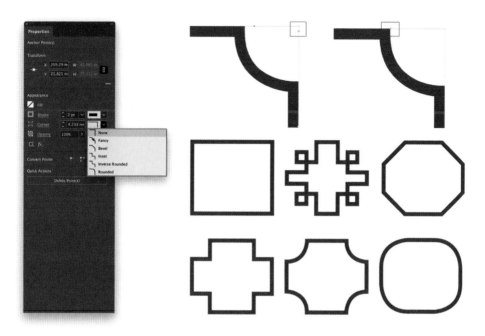

Another way to transform your frames or shapes is to apply corner styles to them. (One of the options is to add rounded corners, but there is another way to create these easily, which is covered on page 68.) Start by creating (or selecting) your frame or shape, and then choose a corner option from the Corner pop-up menu in the Properties panel, or by going to **Object > Corner Options** and selecting a style in the Corner Options dialog. Next, use the Selection Tool **(V)** to select your frame or shape, and then click on the little yellow square that appears on the upper-right side of the frame. This will make it jump to the corners of your shape. If you drag this to the left, it'll increase the size of the corner decoration. Drag it to the right, and the size of the corner decoration is reduced.

How Do I... Combine Shapes or Frames to Create New Ones?

 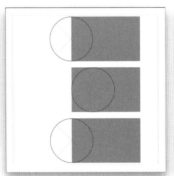 

We've already covered how to create standard shapes and frames for content, but we can actually create some bespoke ones by joining frames or shapes together using the Pathfinder panel **(Window > Object & Layout > Pathfinder)**. The Pathfinder options are as follows:

- Add—Combines selected objects into one shape
- Subtract—Subtracts the frontmost objects from the backmost object
- Intersect—Intersects the shape areas
- Exclude Overlap—Excludes overlapping shape areas
- Minus Back—Subtracts the backmost objects from the frontmost object

In order to apply the Pathfinder options, your shapes must overlap at some point. Then all you need to do is select the shapes and click on one of the options. In the example shown, I have selected a circle and a rectangle and applied the following Pathfinder options (from top to bottom): Add, Subtract, and Minus Back. These are the three options I use the most for shape building in InDesign. You can use these shapes to add color for decoration; insert images or text for a very artsy style; or even wrap text around them (covered in chapter 4). As always with these great tools, play around and see what you can come up with yourself!

How Do I... Convert a Shape (or Frame) to a Different One?

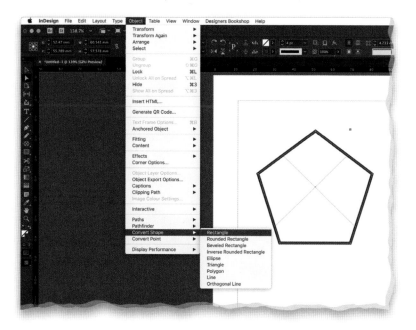

Drawing shapes quickly is great. Maybe you've created a rectangle or polygon, but then you think, "hmm, this feels like it should be a circle." No need to worry! You don't have to delete it and start over; just convert the shape instead. You can easily convert a shape (or frame) to a new shape by selecting it, going to **Object > Convert Shape**, and choosing the shape you need. You can also do this in the Properties panel by clicking on the Convert Shape button (at the bottom of the panel) and choosing your new shape from the pop-up menu, or in the Pathfinder panel by simply selecting the shape you want from the Convert Shape section.

How Do I... Reshape a Shape or Frame with the Pencil Tool?

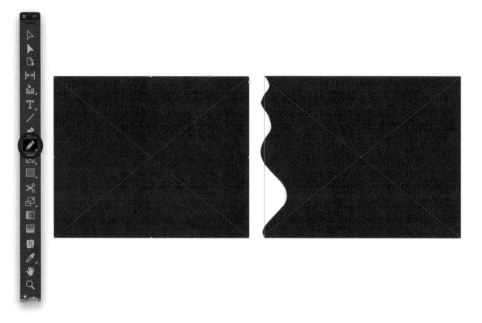

This is an odd technique and it requires a steady hand. Not everything needs to be clean and symmetrical; sometimes a little rough and ready will suffice. If you feel one of your shapes or frames needs to be a little misshapen, shall we say, you can modify it by drawing on the edge of the frame with the Pencil Tool. To do this, just select the shape or frame with the Selection Tool **(V)**, then switch to the Pencil Tool **(N)** and start drawing along the edge from the first point to the finishing point. Be sure to start and finish right on the edge; otherwise it'll look a little funky!

How Do I... Create a Custom Shape with the Pencil Tool?

The Pencil Tool allows you to draw freehand and creates open and closed paths. It's great for creating a more freehand, sketch type of effect. The added benefit is that you can edit what you've drawn. Just select the Pencil Tool **(N)** and begin to draw out your shape. You will see a series of blue dots appear as you draw, and once you release your mouse, the path will take on the attributes of your stroke setting. If the shape is open-ended, there will be a point at each end as well as points along the path. If you press-and-hold the Option (PC: Alt) key *after* you begin drawing, the Pencil Tool cursor will display a small circle to indicate you want to create a closed path. When you are happy with your shape, release the mouse *before* releasing the Option key, and the two open points will be connected.

How Do I... Create a Custom Shape with the Pen Tool?

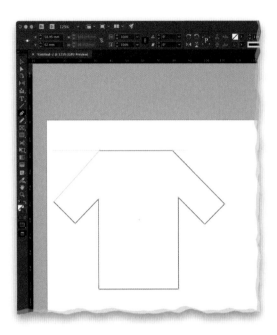

If you know your way around the Pen Tool (one of the most difficult tools in Photoshop, Illustrator, and InDesign to master), you can use it to create your own shapes. I'd say this tip is for the slightly more Pen Tool–experienced person, but feel free to experiment with it to help you understand how it is used. More often than not, you'll be using the basic shapes in your InDesign document. But if you have to create something bespoke, you may want to try this out. Select the Pen Tool **(P)** and click on your document to make your first point. You can make a straight-sided shape quite easily by just clicking again on the location where you want to plant your next point, and so on. Make sure that you close your shape by clicking back on the first point you planted. If you are more experienced with the Pen Tool, you can create curves in your shape, but this requires way more detailed instructions than I can fit on a page (the Pen Tool could fill an entire book itself!). I strongly suggest you find some great Pen Tool tutorials on sites such as KelbyOne.com.

How Do I... Manipulate a Path?

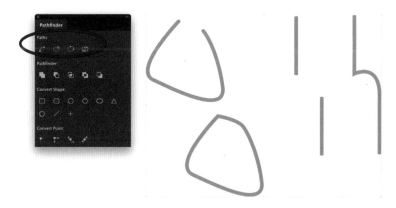

In the Paths section of the Pathfinder panel **(Window > Object & Layout > Pathfinder or Object > Paths)** you'll find some options to help with your shape creation. These are (from left to right in the panel, circled above):

- Join Path—Connects two separate paths. For example, if you create two open-ended shapes and want to connect them, just select a point from one open end and a point from the other, and then click on the Join Path icon. The two selected points will connect.
- Open Path—Opens a closed path. Select a point on a closed path and choose this option to break the connection at that point.
- Close Path—Closes an open path by adding an additional path to bridge the gap between two endpoints.
- Reverse Path—Changes the direction of a path, such as when you have a line with an arrowhead set at one end.

You may not find yourself using these options much, but knowing they are there will help if you are a regular user of vector tools and like to draw directly in InDesign.

? How Do I... Draw Lines In My Document?

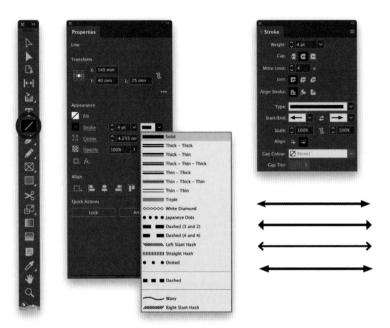

There's a tool in your Toolbar for this and it looks like a line—because that's what it is! With the Line Tool (\) selected, you can drag out a simple straight line in your document. Press-and-hold the Shift key to keep the line horizontal, vertical, or set at a 45-degree angle, and then release the mouse. Before your line will function as a line you need to add a stroke (initially it is only visible as a path). In the Properties panel or the Control panel you can adjust the Fill and Stroke (but with a single line, only the stroke will be applicable), and you can also choose a specific style of line—solid, dashes, dots, hashes, etc.—by clicking on the pop-up menu to the right of the Stroke weight menu. What about adding some nice decorative endpoints to the line, such as arrowheads? You're in luck! Go to **Window > Stroke** to open the Stroke panel, and then click on the Start/End pop-up menus to add arrows or other shapes to the ends of your line. You can adjust the scale of the start/end shape and choose whether the shape sits at the very end of the line or if it is the end of the line. For example, if you've added a triangular arrowhead to your line, either the flat part would sit at the end of the line, or the tip of the triangle would be the end of the line you created. Any colors you choose for the line will apply to these start/end points as well.

? How Do I... Align Objects?

When you're placing a number of objects on a page, it's not always easy to align them, even with Smart Guides switched on. This is where the Align options come into play. You can access the Align options in the Properties panel, Control panel, and Align panel **(Window > Object & Layout > Align)**. All you have to do is select the objects you want to align, and then click on one of the Align icons (circled in the image above). Your options are as follows:

- Align left edges
- Align horizontal centers
- Align right edges
- Align top edges
- Align vertical centers
- Align bottom edges

In the example above, I've selected (from left to right) Align left edges, Align horizontal centers, and Align right edges. Once you've aligned your items, you'll need to look at another aspect of object placement: distribution. That's covered in the tip on page 79.

How Do I... Align Strokes?

InDesign lets you determine where the stroke is aligned on a box or shape. This may sound odd, but if you also use Photoshop and Illustrator, you'll know that you can decide where the stroke sits on an object. You'll find the Align Stroke options in the middle of the Stroke panel **(Window > Stroke)**. By default, the stroke is centered on the path—for example, a 2-point stroke will have 1 point outside the box and 1 point inside the box. With thicker strokes, the placement can really matter. In the image above, there are three boxes that are the exact same size; the only difference is the alignment of the strokes. Because the strokes are set centered, inside, and outside, respectively, it gives the appearance of different-sized squares. It's helpful to use these settings when you're trying to get some precisely measured shapes. I pretty much use the Align Stroke to Inside option all the time to maintain the original size of my shapes, but that's just a personal preference.

How Do I... Create Even Spacing Between Objects?

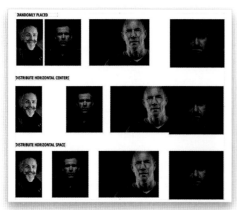  

In the default Align panel **(Window > Object & Layout > Align)**, you have two groups of options from which to choose: Align Objects and Distribute Objects. But there's a third "hidden" option that's way more useful than Distribute Objects. To find this option, open the panel menu at the top-right corner of the Align panel and select Show Options. Now you'll have a new group of options called Distribute Spacing at the bottom of the panel. Imagine you have images that are all different widths and you want to adjust the spacing between them. If you select them all and click on the Distribute horizontal centers icon in the Distribute Objects section, the result would look odd (see the example above). However, if instead you select the now uncovered Distribute horizontal space icon (circled above) in the Distribute Spacing section, you get a more even distribution. Distribute horizontal centers is great for repeated shapes of the same width, but when it comes to shapes with various widths, the Distribute Spacing options are a much better choice. If you want there to be a specific distance between items, put a check mark next to Use Spacing at the bottom of the Align panel, set the distance you require in the field to the right, click the Distribute horizontal space or Distribute vertical space icon, and Bob's your uncle! All of this applies for vertical spacing as well. The Distribute vertical centers option behaves a little better than Distribute horizontal centers, but the best thing about using the Distribute vertical space option is that you can set the distance you want between the images.

How Do I... Use Layers to Organize My Content?

Layers are great for keeping order in your documents. They behave a little differently in InDesign than in Photoshop or Illustrator, but they essentially perform the same function: they enable you to group assets on individual layers within a single document. Even if designers say, "I don't use layers," they really do, as a layer is automatically created when you start adding content onto your page. If I am creating a multipage document, I create a layer for each page to keep the assets for that page together and separate them from the assets on other pages. The layers are automatically color-coded by default, and all the frames on a layer are assigned the color of that layer, which makes it easy to see what group of assets I'm working with at any given time. I can always tell if there is a rogue element on the page or if an element has been placed on the wrong layer because the frame color will be different than the others on that page. This is a really great way to keep tabs on your content. You could always have all of your images on one layer (as in the example above) and all of your text on another—it's all about preference. That's the beauty of layers: you are in control.

? How Do I... Manage My Layers?

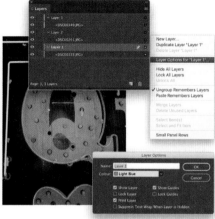

Now that we have our Layers panel open, let's make some changes. In the example above, I have created a layer for each image, and each layer was automatically assigned a color. To change the color of a layer, double-click on the layer to open the Layer Options dialog. Here you can name the layer (highly recommended) and change its color. You also get some options to lock and show layers and guides within that layer. We'll just concentrate on the simple stuff for now to get us started. To move the layers around in the stack (to change the order of overlapping images, for example), just click-and-drag them up or down in the Layers panel. You can also Right-click on a layer to open a context menu that allows you to add a new layer, duplicate that specific layer, delete the layer, open the Layer Options dialog, or select all items within the layer. Clicking on the three little lines in the top-right corner of the Layers panel opens the panel menu, which gives you a few more options in addition to the ones just mentioned. If you click on an element on a page and you can see that it's on the wrong layer, just click on the little colored square to the right of that element's name in the Layers panel and drag it to the correct layer.

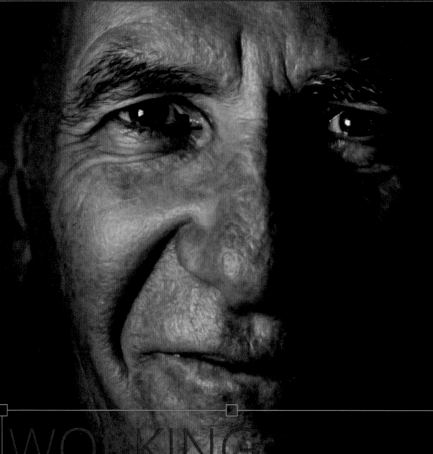

WORKING

WITH TEXT AND TYPE

Chapter 4

How to Work with Text and Type

It's What InDesign Was Made For!

This is the stuff I really love: text and type! I've always been fascinated with type, fonts, lettering, whatever you want to call it. When I was a kid I loved old TV cop and spy shows. Whenever there was a kidnapping, I got excited. Why? Ransom notes! In a talk I do at Photoshop World, I present a slide that says "When I was growing up I wanted to be a…" and I ask the audience what they think. I usually hear "typographer," "author," or "lettering artist," and these are all great suggestions, if I had known at age 7 what those things were. But, for me, it was professional kidnapper, or actually, professional ransom-note maker. I loved that someone was tasked with cutting out letters, keeping them in alphabetical piles, ready to lay out the all-important message. I hoped that whomever it was thought about the layout, the contrasting colors, not duplicating a font, and getting the spacing right. I used to destroy newspapers, catalogs, or anything else with big bold letters and make my own ransom alphabet. Then I would take things from my brother or parents and deliver a well-made ransom note demanding some treat in exchange for the item I stole. This was my introduction to crude desktop publishing at a very young age. As I got older, I discovered the world of dry transfer lettering, known to many as Letraset. This was a new world! I would make covers for cassette tape mixes, my own comics, spy identity cards (a ridiculous notion—I was a spy for goodness sake!), and video-case artwork for shows I recorded off the telly. My point is this: type and lettering is fun, and InDesign is the greatest tool for anyone looking to lay out any kind of document or printed matter. Master the power of InDesign. Even if you never covered yourself in Copydex and newsprint, you can still enjoy the craftsmanship of publishing!

InDesign Fun Fact #4

The origins of InDesign started with a project called Shuksan. It was then named K2, before becoming InDesign 1.0 in 1999.

How Do I... Change the Font?

Changing the font is easy! Use the Type Tool **(T)** to select the text you want to change, and then open the font pop-up menu in the Control panel, Properties panel, or Character panel. You will see sample text next to each font in the menu to help you choose the perfect font. You will also see your highlighted text in the document change in live preview to give you a real-time view of how your design will look.

How Do I... Add Adobe (TypeKit) Fonts to InDesign?

InDesign CC 2019 introduced a brand-new way to easily add new fonts without having to leave the application. With the TypeTool **(T)** selected, open whichever font pop-up menu you prefer to use—in the Control panel, Properties panel, or Character panel—and you'll be presented with the fonts you currently have installed. Click on the Find More tab at the top of the pop-up menu to see the thousands of fonts that are available to you via Adobe Fonts (formerly TypeKit). You can activate any of these fonts immediately with your Creative Cloud subscription. Choose whichever font(s) you'd like to use and click on the Activate icon (looks like a little cloud) to the right of each font. The activated fonts will be available on your computer for all software in which you can type!

How Do I... Filter My Fonts?

Once you have your fonts in your system (let's be honest, we all probably have about ninety percent more than we need, but you can never have too many fonts — said every designer ever), you'll want to be able to quickly find and use the right font for the job. The font pop-up menu enables you to filter your list according to font classification or properties, fonts marked as favorites, recently added fonts, and activated fonts (these will only be Adobe Fonts). To filter your fonts by classification or properties, click on the little funnel icon next to Filters at the top of the font pop-up menu, and then search by classification—Serif, Sans Serif, Decorative, etc.—or by property, which includes weight, height, and width. To mark a font as a favorite, simply hover over the font in the pop-up menu, and then click on the little star icon that appears to the right of it. You can then filter the menu to include only your favorites by clicking on the star icon at the top of the fonts pop-up menu (again next to Filters). Click on the clock icon to view recently added fonts, or click on the cloud with the check mark to view all activated fonts.

How Do I... Find Similar Fonts?

Choosing fonts is one of the hard parts of designing something with text, particularly when you start with no guidelines and a blank canvas. So let's say you start with a font that's not quite right, but you want to find something similar. Just select your text and open the font pop-up menu in the Control panel, Properties panel, or Character panel. Next to your chosen font are a couple of little wavy lines. When you hover over those lines, it will say Show Similar Fonts—click on this to see a list of fonts that are close in style to the one you started with. You can then go ahead and click on a different font to select it. Remember, if you change the font, you may find that your text no longer fits your text frame. In this case, click-and-drag a corner of the frame outward to adjust it.

How Do I... Find and Change a Missing Font?

By default, any type that is using a missing font will be highlighted in pink in your document. If you open up a document and find there is a font missing—maybe you don't have it installed yet or it's not activated—you can quickly find or change it. Select the highlighted type and go to **Type > Find Font**. The Find Font dialog will show you all the fonts in your document and there will be a small warning triangle next to the problem font. To replace the missing font, just go down to the Replace With section and select a new Font Family and Font Style from the respective pop-up menus. Then click on Change All.

If you have a Creative Cloud account, you may find that when you open a document, a dialog will automatically appear warning you of an unactivated font, and you have the option to tell CC to activate it. If you miss this, just log into your Adobe Fonts account and activate the missing font. This will automatically update the document.

How Do I... Change a Font Globally (Without the Use of Styles)?

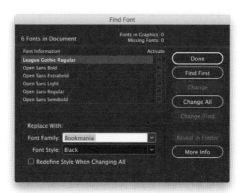

Let's assume you've made a document with multiple pages and all the headers in the document are a set font. You've decided to use a different font for those headings, but you don't want to go through heading by heading to change them. Well, you can adjust the font globally, and you don't even need to create character or paragraph styles to do so (you may not have set any up yet). Go to **Type > Find Font**, and at the top of the Find Font dialog (under Font Information) you'll see a list of the fonts used in your current document. Click on the font you want to replace (in this case, League Gothic Regular), and then go down to the Replace With section and use the pop-up menus to choose the Font Family and Font Style you want to use instead (we'll change to Bookmania). Now click the Change All button, and all instances of League Gothic Regular in your document will be replaced with Bookmania. It's that simple! You'll also be presented with this option if you open a document containing a font that is not installed on your system (see previous tip).

How Do I... Resize My Text Quickly?

When it comes to quickly resizing your type, you can use an easy shortcut to save yourself from having to adjust a menu in the Properties panel or Character panel over and over again. To increase the size of your type by 2 points, highlight the text and press **Command-Shift-> (PC: Ctrl-Shift->)**. Keep pressing the arrow key to keep increasing the size. This is perfect for making those quick adjustments. To make your highlighted type shrink by 2 points, press **Command-Shift-< (PC: Ctrl-Shift-<)**. What if you want to work with even larger increments? You may want to jump 4 points, 6 points, 8 points, or even 10 points every time you use this shortcut. If you want to super-size your text, go to **InDesign (PC: Edit) > Preferences > Units & Increments**. In the Keyboard Increments section you'll see that Size/Leading is currently set to 2 pt, which is the default amount. Enter 4, 6, 8, 10, or higher to increase/decrease your text size in larger increments when using this shortcut. Just remember to switch it back to 2 when you don't need gigantic text.

How Do I... Get the Text Frame to Resize as I Type?

Type has to be applied in a text frame, and sometimes not all of your type will fit in the frame you've created. You then have to spend time resizing the text frame as you work. But there's a really cool trick to get around this issue, and when I showed it at Photoshop World, everyone went "whoa!" (even Scott Kelby!). It has been right there in InDesign all this time! To make the text frame resize automatically as you add text, just go to **Object > Text Frame Options**. In the Text Frame Options dialog click on the Auto-Size tab, and then select **Height Only** from the Auto-Sizing pop-up menu. In the square box below, select the top-middle option (the little arrow pointing downward). This means the text will always start at the top of the frame and work down. Click OK, and now your text box will resize as you type. To ensure this happens every time, apply this setting before you create your document (with no documents open), and it will become the default for that document every time you create a text frame. Play around with some of the other settings here too—you may find another useful default for placing your text.

How Do I... Check Spelling in My Document?

Much like word-processing programs such as Microsoft Word, InDesign has the ability to spellcheck selected text or all text in documents. To check the spelling in your document, go to **Edit > Spelling > Check Spelling**. Open the Search pop-up menu at the bottom of the Check Spelling dialog and choose whether to Search All Documents (all open documents), the current Document, the currently selected Story, To End Of Story (checks from the current cursor insertion point), or just the current Selection. Use the Check Spelling dialog to change or ignore any misspelled words. If you use words that are not in the built-in dictionary, you can add them to the User Dictionary. Make sure User Dictionary is selected from the Add To pop-up menu, and then click Add. You can also have InDesign automatically check spelling as you work. Go to **Edit > Spelling > Dynamic Spelling** to enable automatic spellcheck. This feature doesn't auto-correct spelling, but it will notify you of misspelled words as you type, or when you paste unchecked text into your document, by adding a wavy line under any offending words.

You can quickly check the word count of your document in the Info panel. Go to **Window > Info** to open the panel, and at the bottom of the panel you will see the number of characters, words, lines, and paragraphs in your text. You can leave this panel open as you work, and it will update as you type.

How Do I... Use the Story Editor?

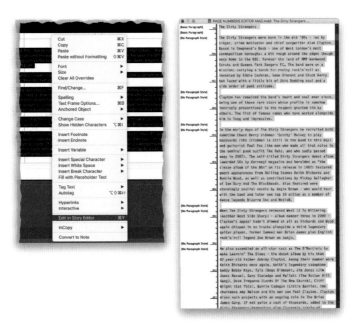

The Story Editor can be selected by Right-clicking in your text frame and choosing **Edit in Story Editor** from the menu. The reason this exists is so that you can edit large chunks of text in a simple text-only format, much like an old word processor. Just place the cursor anywhere in the text and you can start making changes or additions to your text without worrying about frame sizes or pages. This is especially useful when you're working with linked or threaded text (see page 105 for how to link text boxes).

How Do I... Adjust Leading and Tracking?

If you want to adjust the leading or tracking for your text, just open up the Character panel **(Type > Character)**—this is where these settings live. It's usually a good idea to zoom into the text so you can see the effect better as you change the settings. First, highlight the text you want to adjust. In the Character panel you are looking for the two pop-up menus near the middle of the panel on the right side. The first—Leading—shows two A's stacked vertically. This will adjust the space between lines of text. Click the up arrow to increase the leading in the highlighted text, or open the pop-up menu to select a value. The Tracking icon shows the letters VA with a horizontal double-headed arrow underneath. Increasing the tracking value will increase the space between the letters.

How Do I... Change Text Alignment?

The Dirty Strangers were born in the mid '80s – led by singer, prime motivator and chief songwriter Alan Clayton. Based in Shepherd's Bush – one of West London's most cosmopolitan boroughs: a bit rough around the edges though once home to the BBC, forever the land of HMP Wormwood Scrubs and Queens Park Rangers FC. **ALIGN LEFT**	The Dirty Strangers were born in the mid '80s – led by singer, prime motivator and chief songwriter Alan Clayton. Based in Shepherd's Bush – one of West London's most cosmopolitan boroughs: a bit rough around the edges though once home to the BBC, forever the land of HMP Wormwood Scrubs and Queens Park Rangers FC. **ALIGN CENTER**	The Dirty Strangers were born in the mid '80s – led by singer, prime motivator and chief songwriter Alan Clayton. Based in Shepherd's Bush – one of West London's most cosmopolitan boroughs: a bit rough around the edges though once home to the BBC, forever the land of HMP Wormwood Scrubs and Queens Park Rangers FC. **ALIGN RIGHT**	
The Dirty Strangers were born in the mid '80s – led by singer, prime motivator and chief songwriter Alan Clayton. Based in Shepherd's Bush - one of West London's most cosmopolitan boroughs: a bit rough around the edges though once home to the BBC, forever the land of HMP Wormwood Scrubs and Queens Park Rangers FC. **JUSTIFY WITH LAST LINE ALIGNED LEFT**	The Dirty Strangers were born in the mid '80s – led by singer, prime motivator and chief songwriter Alan Clayton. Based in Shepherd's Bush - one of West London's most cosmopolitan boroughs: a bit rough around the edges though once home to the BBC, forever the land of HMP Wormwood Scrubs and Queens Park Rangers FC. **JUSTIFY WITH LAST LINE ALIGNED CENTER**	The Dirty Strangers were born in the mid '80s – led by singer, prime motivator and chief songwriter Alan Clayton. Based in Shepherd's Bush - one of West London's most cosmopolitan boroughs: a bit rough around the edges though once home to the BBC, forever the land of HMP Wormwood Scrubs and Queens Park Rangers FC. **JUSTIFY WITH LAST LINE ALIGNED RIGHT**	The Dirty Strangers were born in the mid '80s – led by singer, prime motivator and chief songwriter Alan Clayton. Based in Shepherd's Bush – one of West London's most cosmopolitan boroughs: a bit rough around the edges though once home to the BBC, forever the land and Queens Park Rangers FC. **JUSTIFY ALL LINES**
The Dirty Strangers were born in the mid '80s – led by singer, prime motivator and chief songwriter Alan Clayton. Based in Shepherd's Bush - one of West London's most cosmopolitan boroughs: a bit rough around the edges though once home to the BBC, forever the land of HMP Wormwood Scrubs and Queens Park Rangers FC. **ALIGN AWAY FROM SPINE (LEFT PAGE)**	The Dirty Strangers were born in the mid '80s – led by singer, prime motivator and chief songwriter Alan Clayton. Based in Shepherd's Bush - one of West London's most cosmopolitan boroughs: a bit rough around the edges though once home to the BBC, forever the land of HMP Wormwood Scrubs and Queens Park Rangers FC. **ALIGN TOWARDS SPINE (LEFT PAGE)**	The Dirty Strangers were born in the mid '80s – led by singer, prime motivator and chief songwriter Alan Clayton. Based in Shepherd's Bush - one of West London's most cosmopolitan boroughs: a bit rough around the edges though once home to the BBC, forever the land of HMP Wormwood Scrubs and Queens Park Rangers FC. **ALIGN TOWARDS SPINE (RIGHT PAGE)**	The Dirty Strangers were born in the mid '80s – led by singer, prime motivator and chief songwriter Alan Clayton. Based in Shepherd's Bush - one of West London's most cosmopolitan boroughs: a bit rough around the edges though once home to the BBC, forever the land of HMP Wormwood Scrubs and Queens Park Rangers FC. **ALIGN AWAY FROM SPINE (RIGHT PAGE)**

This is a simple but important step when laying out text in your document. A lot of times designers will just use left-aligned or centered text and ignore the other alignment options. Don't do that! The others are just as important. Alignment can be adjusted in the Paragraph panel, Properties panel, or Control panel. Choose an alignment option before you insert your text to make it the default. If you want to change the alignment of your text, highlight the text and click on a new option. The following options are available (see image for examples, in the order listed):

- Align left
- Align center
- Align right

- Justify with last line aligned left
- Justify with last line aligned center
- Justify with last line aligned right
- Justify all lines

- Align towards spine
- Align away from spine

In the bottom row of paragraphs above, you can see that depending on where I placed the text, it automatically aligned away from or toward the spine.

How Do I... Change the Case of My Type?

Changing case in InDesign doesn't mean retyping everything. Just select the type that needs to be changed, go to **Type > Change Case**, and select from UPPERCASE, lowercase, Title Case, and Sentence case. It really is that simple.

Now, moving along...

How Do I... Insert a Glyph?

The Dirty Strangers were born in the mid '80s – led by singer, prime motivator and chief songwriter Alan Clayton. Based in Shepherd's Bush – one of West London's most cosmopolitan boroughs: a bit rough around the edges though once home to the BBC, forever the land of HMP Wormwood Scrubs and Queens Park Rangers FC.™

Glyphs are also known as special characters. These include bullets, checkboxes, ornaments, and accented characters. It's really simple to add a glyph to your text. Using the Type Tool **(T)**, insert your cursor where you want the glyph to appear, and then select **Type > Glyphs**. This will open the Glyphs panel, which shows the glyphs available for the font you currently have selected. Click on the Show pop-up menu to find a list of sorting options, including OpenType attributes, symbols, numbers, ornaments, fractions, swashes, ligatures, and more. Search for the glyph you'd like to use and double-click on it to insert it into your text. In the example above, I chose to add a trademark symbol (™) after the words "Queen's Park Rangers." In the Glyphs panel, I chose **Symbols** from the Show menu, located the ™, and double-clicked on it. This inserted the symbol into the space, and there you have it! Any recently used glyphs are displayed at the top of the Glyphs panel. This comes in handy when you're using the same glyph frequently.

?How Do I... Insert Placeholder Text?

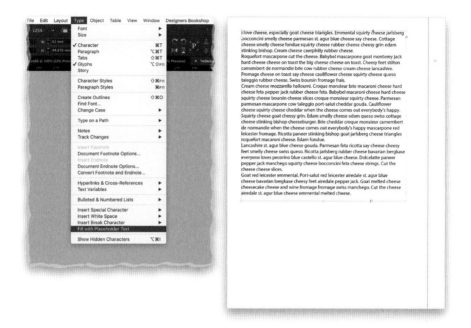

Sometimes you need to use placeholder text so you can get a sense of how your layout will look with text in it. The industry standard, and InDesign default, is good old lorem ipsum. To use placeholder text in a document, all you need to do is create a text frame and go to **Type > Fill with Placeholder Text**.

TIP: CHANGE THE DEFAULT PLACEHOLDER TEXT

Lorem ipsum is boring. But are we stuck with it? No! We can replace it with any text. There are websites where you can get alternative types of placeholder text, such as:

- http://www.cheeseipsum.co.uk
- https://baconipsum.com
- http://doctoripsum.com
- https://pirateipsum.me
- And my favorite: https://slipsum.com (Warning: This website does contain profanity...it wouldn't be Sam L. Jackson if it didn't! Remember, if you use the profanity version for fun, make sure you change it before doing a presentation!)

Paste the new text into a text editor—no formatting, just plain text—then save this file with the name "placeholder.txt." Move this file into the InDesign application root folder. You won't even need to restart InDesign; the next time you use Fill with Placeholder Text, you'll see your new placeholder text instead of lorem ipsum.

How Do I... Insert Text from a Word Document?

Not many people know this, but you can place an entire Word document as content in InDesign. Many people just copy and paste the content from the Word doc into the InDesign doc, and you can do that, but this tip explains how to place the actual document. Go to **File > Place** and locate the Word document you want to use. Make sure you check the Import Options checkbox at the bottom of the Place dialog, or this won't work properly (at least not in a way that gives you any control). Click Open, and you'll get a dialog called Microsoft Word Import Options ([name of doc]. docx). We'll focus on the Formatting section in the lower half of the dialog, which offers you two choices for dealing with imported text:

Remove Styles and Formatting from Text and Tables—This will strip all the formatting from your Word document and use whatever default styles you have set in your InDesign document.

Preserve Styles and Formatting from Text and Tables—This will maintain all formatting you have applied in your Word document. Here's the handy part: it also gives you the option to import your Word styles.

Once you've made your selection, click OK and your cursor will be loaded with the Word document. Now click anywhere in your InDesign document to place the text from the Word doc.

? How Do I... Type on a Path?

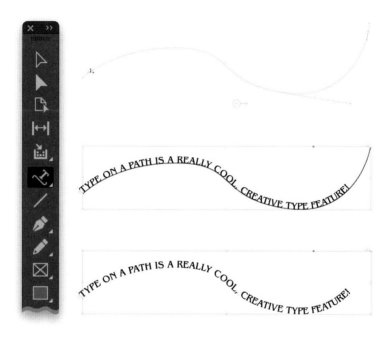

If you are trying to add type to a curve—such as one created with the Pen Tool **(P)**, as in the example shown above—draw out your curve, or make a shape using one of the shape tools, and then change the Type Tool to the Type on a Path Tool. (*Tip:* To get to the Type on a Path Tool, click-and-hold on the Type Tool in the Toolbar to open the flyout menu, and then select the Type on a Path Tool from the menu; or press **Shift-T**.) When you hold the cursor over the path on which you wish to type, it will change and show a small + sign. When you see this, click once to place the cursor. Now you can type out your text and it will follow along the path. Remember, the harsher the path the worse the text will look as it moves along the path. Using caution and knowing why you are adding the type on the path is critical to the look and feel of the design.

How Do I... Customize My Type on a Path?

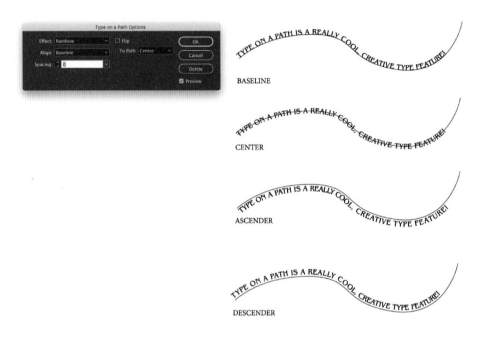

Want more control over how your type on a path works? Create a path, then add some text. There's an additional trick to give you some extra options. Just go to the Toolbar and double-click directly on the Type on a Path Tool to bring up its options. One of the clever little options is the Effect pop-up menu, which you can use to apply different type-on-a-path effects, even after the type has already been placed. Caveat: I didn't say they'd all look good, just that they'll work. It all comes down to the font and positioning of the text, but you can create some cool effects with the right recipe of font and effect. You will also see alignment and spacing values. The Spacing value compensates for the way characters fan out around a curve or sharp angle—the higher values remove any extra space between the characters that are positioned on the angles or sharp curves. This has no effect on the characters positioned on the straighter segments. To change the spacing of characters anywhere along the path, select them, and then apply kerning or tracking via the Character panel. The Align value determines where on the path the type will sit: Baseline, Center, Ascender, or Descender.

?How Do I... Apply Bullets or Numbers (or Letters) to My Text?

We all love lists, and we love good old bullet points just as much! To emphasize a list by adding bullets or numbers (or letters), highlight the text and open up the Properties panel **(Window > Properties)**. Near the bottom of the panel are icons for Bullets and Numbering. Choosing either will format your list and add exactly what it says. Click on the Options button to open the Bullets and Numbering dialog, where you can fine-tune your character style and bullet or number position. You can choose a different symbol to use for your bullets, or you can switch from numbers to letters or Roman numerals.

How Do I... Turn Off Automatic Hyphenation?

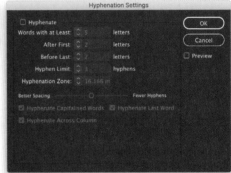

Automatic hyphenation is one of those things that drives me nuts until I remember to turn it off. You can turn it off while you're working on a document, but I think it's better to turn it off before you start a new document because that way it'll stay off. If you've already started working on your document, highlight all of your text by pressing **Command-A (PC: Ctrl-A)** (assuming you are getting hyphenation), and then go over to the far right side of the Control panel and click on the icon with three horizontal lines, sometimes referred to as "the burger," directly below the little gear icon. Select Hyphenation from the pop-up menu to open the Hyphenation Settings dialog. Uncheck the Hyphenation checkbox at the top of the dialog to turn this feature off. If you want to leave it turned on, you can use the settings in this dialog to control how it is applied. I don't use hyphenation in most of the work I do (aside from this book, natch), but the option is there for those who need it!

How Do I... Make Text Flow/Thread from One Frame to the Next?

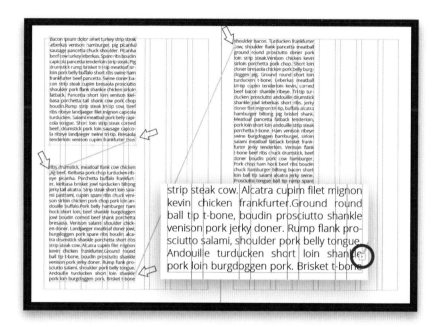

When creating a document, you may want to have your text frames spread out over different pages, but you need the text to flow from one frame to the next. You can place the text independently in each frame, but when you start editing you will be cutting and pasting all over the place and it can get messy. To make your text flow between frames, you must first connect them. When text flows between connected frames it's called threaded text (or linked text frames or linked text boxes—it's all the same thing). These connected frames can be on the same page or across spreads, or on any other page in the document. The important thing to know when you begin is that each text frame has an "in port" and an "out port," which are used to make connections to the other text frames. These ports are found near the top-left and bottom-right corners of the text frames, respectively. Each one looks like a small box, sometimes with a symbol in it. If you have an empty in port or out port box, it means you are at the beginning or end of a set of text. If a port has an arrow in it, it means the frame is linked to another one. If you see red plus sign (+) in the out port, it means there is more text available that will not fit into the frame. You can create a new text frame for this text by clicking on the red + and drawing out a frame. If you don't have any text inserted, but you still want to create threaded frames, just click on the first frame's out port, and then click on the next frame's in port. Once you start to add text, it will automatically flow from one frame to the next, and the next, and so on, depending on how many you have linked.

How Do I... Wrap Text Around an Image or Shape?

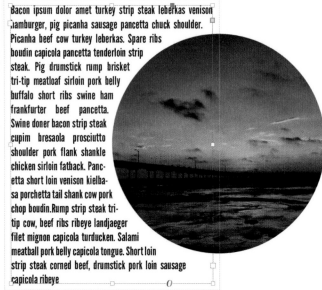

Bacon ipsum dolor amet turkey strip steak leberkas venison hamburger, pig picanha sausage pancetta chuck shoulder. Picanha beef cow turkey leberkas. Spare ribs boudin capicola pancetta tenderloin strip steak. Pig drumstick rump brisket tri-tip meatloaf sirloin pork belly buffalo short ribs swine ham frankfurter beef pancetta. Swine doner bacon strip steak cupim bresaola prosciutto shoulder pork flank shankle chicken sirloin fatback. Pancetta short loin venison kielbasa porchetta tail shank cow pork chop boudin.Rump strip steak tri-tip cow, beef ribs ribeye landjaeger filet mignon capicola turducken. Salami meatball pork belly capicola tongue. Short loin strip steak corned beef, drumstick pork loin sausage capicola ribeye

Wrapping text around a shape is not as complicated as you'd think because there's a panel for that very thing—the Text Wrap panel **(Window > Text Wrap)**! You can get the text to behave in a few different ways. Start by selecting both the text and shape together (click-and-drag the cursor over both, or click on one and then Shift-click on the other), and then click on one of the Text Wrap icons at the top of the panel.

No text wrap

Wrap around bounding box—The text will wrap around the frame of the shape.

Wrap around object shape—The text will wrap around the shape (didn't they name that perfectly?!), so whether it's a standard shape or an unusual shape that has a clipping path, the text will wrap around that path.

Jump object—When the text reaches the top of the shape or frame, it will jump over it and continue below it, leaving the sides clear.

Jump to next column—Once the text reaches the shape, it will jump to the next available column.

The pop-up menus directly below the Text Wrap icons enable you to control the gap between the shape or frame and the text. Select the Top, Bottom, Left, and Right Offset individually, or click on the chain-link icon in the middle of the menus to make all offset settings the same. The Wrap To menu gives you the opportunity to choose which side or sides of the shape the text is placed on.

? How Do I... Change the Color of My Type?

Changing the color of type is simple enough. There are multiple places where you can select your color, but I tend to use the Swatches panel **(Window > Color > Swatches)** most often. Just select the type you want to change, and then click on your color of choice in the panel and it will be applied to the highlighted text. (You can also select a text color via the Control panel by clicking on the arrow next to the text Fill icon to open a menu of swatches; or you can select a color in the Properties panel by clicking on the T under Appearance.) If you want to change the color of all text within a text frame, then simply select the frame and click on the little T at the top of the Swatches panel. (*Note:* It is important to click on the T because if the little square to the left of it is selected, your color will be applied to the entire frame as a fill color; the T lets you know you are changing the color of the type. You'll make that mistake a few times before you get the hang of it!) Now when you select a color, it will be applied to all text within the selected frame. If you don't want to use one of the available swatches, you can create a new color by double-clicking on the text Fill icon (colored T) in the Control panel to open up the Color Picker. Either select a color with the crosshair selector or type in any predetermined values for RGB, CMYK, Lab, or HEX, and then click OK.

How Do I... Create a Drop Cap?

Sometimes you want to give your text an extra little something fancy, and drop caps are a good way to do this. To begin your text with a drop cap, select and highlight the first letter of the text, and then open the Paragraph panel **(Type > Paragraph)**. About two-thirds of the way down the panel, just above the Shading checkbox, is the Drop Cap Number of Lines menu (hover over the little icon with the vertical double-headed arrow next to an A to make sure you've found the correct menu). Enter the number 2 to make the letter drop down two lines. Note the number 1 in the Drop Cap One or More Characters menu to the right. This menu allows you to increase the number of characters that drop down two lines. It wouldn't look pretty, but you could do it! Once you have applied your drop cap, you can go ahead and apply some additional styling to the letter—maybe make it Extra Bold and change the color.

ROCK'N'ROLL

When a solid color just isn't enough for your type, how can you add something cool like a sexy gradient? Yes, I said sexy for impact. Adding a gradient is as simple as selecting the text to which you want to apply the gradient, opening up the Gradient panel **(Window > Color > Gradient)**, and clicking on the gradient icon in the upper-left corner of the panel. This applies the default black-to-white gradient. Now click once on the little box below the left end of the gradient bar at the bottom of the panel, and then double-click on the Type color icon in the Control panel to bring up the Color Picker dialog. You can select any color for your gradient, but here's a tip: if you want to select an existing color in your document, just click-and-hold on the little eyedropper in the Color Picker dialog and drag it over to the color in your document, then release. Press OK, and then repeat the steps for the other end of the gradient. You can rotate the gradient path by typing a degree value into the Angle field in the Gradient panel, and you can click on Reverse to switch the colors around. Use the Type pop-up menu to select a Linear or Radial gradient.

A drop shadow is only going to work effectively on large text. To add the shadow, use the Selection Tool **(V)** to select your text block, and then go to **Object > Effects > Drop Shadow**. Before you change any settings in the Effects dialog, make sure you check the Preview checkbox so you can see a live preview of the effect as you make your selections. Then make sure that Drop Shadow is checked in the list of effects on left side of the dialog (it should be checked already if you selected **Drop Shadow** from the Object > Effects menu). You can then change the Blending Mode and Opacity, and adjust the position and angle of the shadow. Click OK when you're done. Just remember that when it comes to effects like drop shadows, just because you can doesn't always mean you should! Also note that in InDesign a drop shadow (or an effect) can only be applied to the entire contents of the frame— in this instance, the text frame. In other words, you can't just select one word within a text frame and apply a drop shadow to it. To do that, you would have to place that word into a separate text frame.

How Do I... Add Paragraph Shading?

The Dirty Strangers were born in the mid '80s – led by singer, prime motivator and chief songwriter Alan Clayton. Based in Shepherd's Bush – one of West London's most cosmopolitan boroughs: a bit rough around the edges though once home to the BBC, forever the land of HMP Wormwood Scrubs and Queens Park Rangers FC... The band were on a mission: carrying a torch for rootsy rock'n'roll as invented by Eddie Cochran, Gene Vincent and Chuck Berry but laced with a little bit of Otis Redding soul and a side order of punk attitude.

Highlight the text to which you want to add shading, and then put a check mark next to Shading in the Paragraph panel. Use the Shading pop-up menu to choose your color. It's as simple as that! This is great for making text stand out in a document. Maybe you have some callout text you'd like to highlight or a tip you want to emphasize. You can also add a border to your shading by checking the Border box and choosing a color from the pop-up menu.

How Do I... Set My Own Defaults?

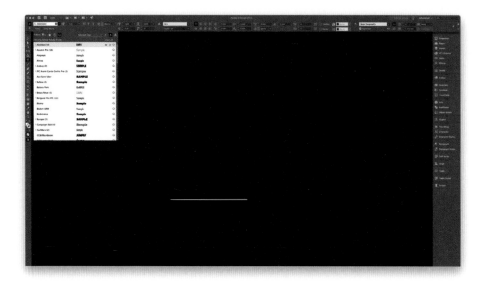

My default font is always Minion Pro. Do you want your default font to be different than the one InDesign has chosen? Do you want the default stroke to be .5 instead of 1 point? Do you want all your text to be last-line justified? Do you want to automatically turn off hyphenation? You can change many of these defaults, but there's a trick to this—well, not exactly a trick, but just something to remember to do before you open any new document (assuming you don't have styles set yet). To set your own global defaults, you just have to set them all when there is no document open at all. That's correct, close all your open documents, every single one of them. Then make whatever changes you want to your settings, and these new settings will become your defaults when you open a new file. This catches me out every time, and I am a seasoned user! You'll thank me for this one! (Well, I hope you thank me for a lot of these tips.)

How Do I... Set My Preferred Character and Paragraph Styles?

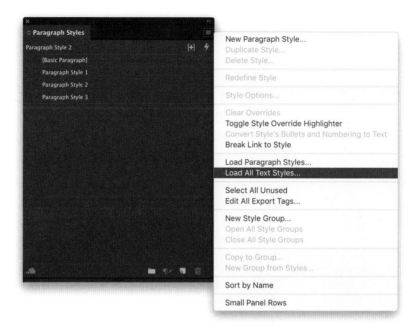

We have covered how to set defaults for your font, stroke, hyphenation, and other settings, but you can also set your preferred character and paragraph styles. The easiest way to do this is to import styles from an existing document. First, make sure you have no documents open. This is always the most important step for setting style preferences. Then go to **Type > Character Styles** or **Paragraph Styles** (this tip works for either). From the panel menu, choose **Load All Text Styles**. Navigate your way to the existing document that contains the styles you want to use as your preferences, and then click Open. It's as simple as that; the styles from that document are imported, and those styles are now set as your preferred paragraph and character styles. You can still go in and make a couple of tweaks, but this is a great way to set these styles quickly. If I have a specific set of requirements for a document, I sometimes make a dummy document that contains all my styles, and then I save it in Dropbox. Then if I am on the road and need to make a document using those styles, I can pull in the ones set in my dummy document.

?) How Do I... Switch to the Type Tool Quickly?

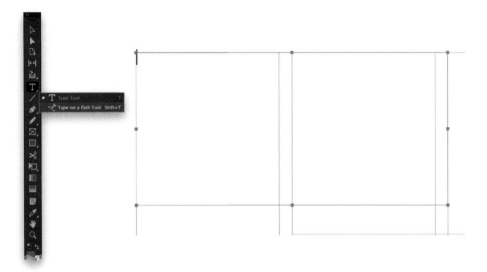

If you're working on a document with multiple text frames, and you want to quickly enter some text in a particular frame, you don't have to go to the Toolbar to switch to the Type Tool. Just hit **T** to swap to the Type Tool, and then single-click inside any visible text frame. This will immediately switch you to the Type Tool and your cursor will be in place, ready for you to type away or paste text inside the frame.

When the Type Tool **(T)** is active, you can quickly switch between character options and paragraph options in the Control panel by pressing **Command-Option-7 (PC: Ctrl-Alt-7)**. This toggles the two layouts. Once you become a fast-fingered InDesign ninja, you'll be using all kinds of shortcuts, and this will be one you use without thinking. (*Note:* See page 276 for instructions on how to find a complete list of default and custom keyboard shortcuts for InDesign.)

When you need to quickly change a value in the Character panel, don't try to insert your cursor into the tiny field, delete the current value, and then type your new value—instead, you can just click on the icon for the attribute you want to change, and the field will be highlighted. Now all you have to do is type in the new amount. This tip may seem like a small one, but if you're frequently adjusting values in the Character panel, it starts to make a big difference. Want to go even quicker? Many times just having to type in those values takes too long and is too fiddly. Once the value is highlighted, speed things up by using the up/down arrow keys on your keyboard to quickly increase or decrease the amount. When you've got the value you need, press **Return (PC: Enter)**.

How Do I... Turn One Text Column into Multiple Columns?

When adding large amounts of text to a document, you can quickly convert a single column of text into multiple columns by switching to the Selection Tool (**[V]**; that's the black arrow in the Toolbar), pressing-and-holding the Option (PC: Alt) key, and double-clicking on the text frame to open the Text Frame Options dialog. In the Columns section, use the Number pop-up menu to choose how many columns you'd like your text split into. These columns will sit within a single text frame. Make sure you click on the Preview checkbox for a live preview of how your columns will look in the document. When you're satisfied, click OK.

When you find yourself working with type frequently or editing a lot of text, you can save a ton of time by learning some simple shortcuts for selecting type. Try these on for size to quickly start selecting your text:

- To select an entire word: double-click on it.
- To select characters to the left of where your text cursor is located: press **Shift-left arrow key**. Every press of the arrow key adds one more character to the selection.
- To select characters to the right of where your text cursor is located: press **Shift-right arrow key**. Every press of the arrow key adds one character to the selection.
- To select a whole line of text: triple-click on it.
- To select an entire paragraph: quadruple-click on it (yep, that's four clicks).
- To select the line in which your text cursor is currently located: press **Command-Shift-\ (PC: Ctrl-Shift-\)**.

By just using these six simple shortcuts, you'll save more time every time you need to select text!

How Do I... See the Text I'm Moving While I'm Moving It?

This might sound like an odd tip, but it can be useful. If you click-and-drag a text frame, the text inside vanishes until you release your mouse. If you can be patient, just click-and-hold on the text frame, and wait a second before you start to drag it. Once you do start dragging, you'll see the text displayed as you drag, instead of an empty frame. Because InDesign is rendering the text and displaying it live as you drag, it moves a tad slower, and any effects (such as the drop shadow in this example) may appear pixelated, but that will revert once you release the frame. However, if you want to reposition text frames quickly, just click and immediately drag, and InDesign will display only the frame (and move at a quicker pace).

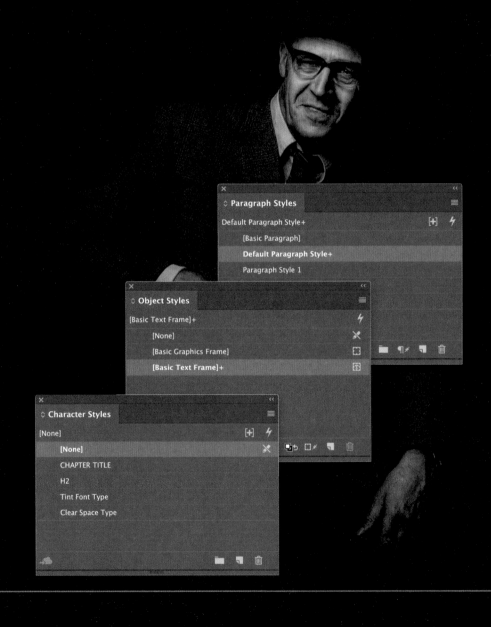

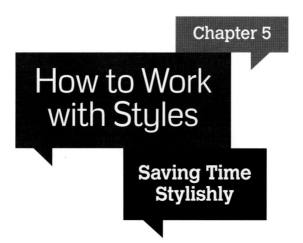

Chapter 5

How to Work with Styles

Saving Time Stylishly

In the last chapter intro I spoke about my love of type. I talked about how I sat and did everything manually, over and over again. The beauty of styles in InDesign, and in fact, in any of the Adobe apps where type is used, is that you can define set styles for your type to ensure uniformity across your characters and paragraphs. Being able to set all your style guides for documents means you can create and save multiple styles for all documents, all projects, and all clients. You can also do the same for objects—frames, shapes, and images—in InDesign. It requires you to put in some effort at the start, but over the course of creating multiple documents you'll definitely reap the benefits of this powerful, time-saving feature. I'll hold my hand up; there's been many a time when I have had to do a quick and dirty job, jumping in and creating content with careless abandonment and ignoring styles. But man, when I have to go back to that job and edit or create additional content without my styles set up…well, I could take myself down one of those shady looking alleyways from a seedy '70s cop show and duff myself up and leave myself in a dumpster. What's with all this law enforcement, '70s cop show, and espionage talk in my chapter intros you wonder? Okay, I admit, I wanted to be either Starsky or Napoleon Solo growing up. Who wouldn't want a friend called Huggy Bear or Illya Kuryakin (try saying that, let alone spelling it correctly!)? Mike Kubeisy, a fellow Photoshop World instructor and friend of KelbyOne, works as the chief photographer on the show NCIS. He gets to work with David McCallum (Illya Kuryakin) and says he's a very nice chap. I am glad he is. He was a blooming great spy for U.N.C.L.E.!

InDesign Fun Fact #5

There are now at least 86 InDesign User Groups in 36 countries with over 51,000 members—we're a big community!

How Do I... Find the Styles Panels?

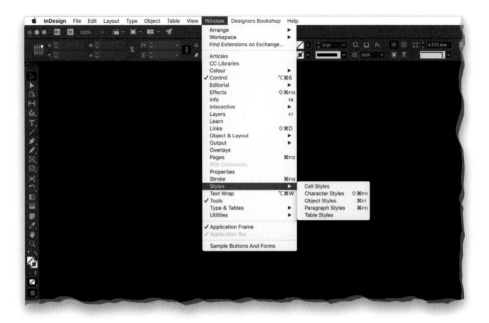

Go to **Window > Styles** and you will be presented with the available styles panels:

- Cell Styles
- Character Styles
- Object Styles
- Paragraph Styles
- Table Styles

Select whichever panel you want to open, and it will appear in your workspace. Repeat the process to open another panel. Any panel that has a check mark next to its name in the menu is already open. Once you've opened a panel you can leave it floating or dock it with your other panels. If you are using styles in your document it's a good idea to stack all of the styles panels together.

How Do I... Create a Character Style?

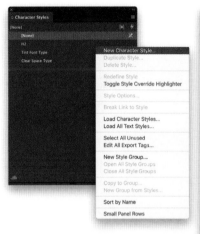
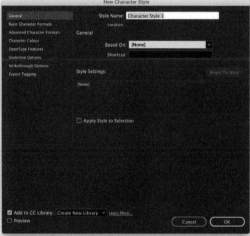

The Character Styles panel is used to create, name, and apply character styles to text within a paragraph. These styles are saved with the document for which they were created, and will be displayed in the Character Styles panel each time you open that particular document. To create a style, you can either use the characteristics of type you've already formatted on the page, or build a new style from scratch via the Character Styles panel menu. To do the former, make sure your cursor is positioned within the text you're using to create the style, click on the panel menu icon in the top-right corner of Character Styles panel, and select **New Character Style**. In the New Character Style dialog, go down to the Style Settings section to review the attributes you've chosen. If you want to tweak anything, click on the options in the menu on the left side of the panel to access various text attribute settings. Once you're satisfied, click OK, and your new style will appear in the Character Styles panel. Repeat the process for any other styles you'd like to create, and then save the document. You can also copy the styled text and paste it into a new document, and the styles will be carried over with the type, or you can import the styles into another document (see page 130). Whenever I start a project, I create a new document and lay out all of my various text elements—headers, body text, captions, etc.—in separate text frames. Then I manually apply the styling—font, size, weight, color, etc.—to each text element. When I'm satisfied, I create character styles for each type of text.

How Do I... Apply a Character Style?

This is really easy to do. Highlight the text to which you want to apply a character style, then go to the Character Style panel and either click on the style name or Right-click on it and choose **Apply "[name of style]."** This will automatically apply the style to the selected text.

How Do I... Create a Paragraph Style?

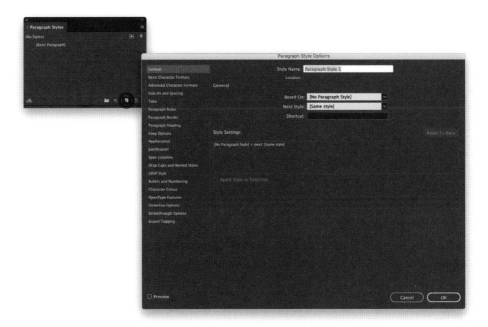

Paragraph styles let you apply and globally update text formatting to entire paragraphs, not just to selected characters. They comprise all the elements of your text formatting, so in addition to text attributes such as font, size, color, and weight, paragraph styles also include paragraph attributes like indents, tabs, alignment, and hyphenation. However, you can override some elements with character styles. To create a basic paragraph style from scratch, make sure none of your text is currently selected, and click on the Create New Style icon at the bottom of the Paragraph Styles panel (it looks like a sheet of paper with a folded corner). Double-click on the newly created style—Paragraph Style 1—and InDesign will open the Paragraph Style Options dialog. (*Note:* If you press-and-hold the **Options (PC: Alt) key** when you click on the Create New Style icon, you'll create the style and open the Paragraph Style Options dialog with one click.) We're just going to create a basic style, so ignore the other settings for now. Click on Basic Character Formats on the left side of the dialog and set a font style for your basic paragraph. Give your style a name and click OK. You have now created a basic paragraph style. You can also create a new paragraph style from a line of text that has already been formatted. Select the formatted text and click on the Create New Style icon at the bottom of the Paragraph Styles panel. It's as simple as that—it takes all the attributes of the selected text and applies them to the style. You can rename the style by double-clicking on its name.

How Do I... Apply a Paragraph Style?

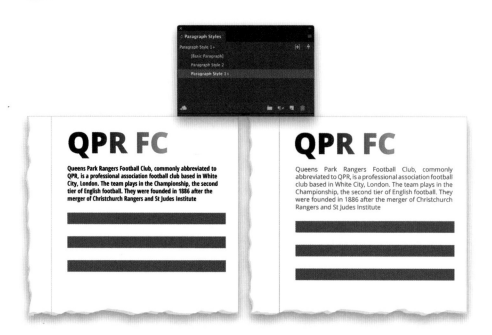

Insert your cursor in the paragraph to which you'd like to apply a paragraph style. (*Note:* Unlike when you're applying a character style, you do not have to highlight all of the text to which you want to apply a paragraph style. You only need to insert your cursor somewhere within the paragraph, or just select the text frame—this won't overwrite any existing character styles.) Go to the Paragraph Styles panel and either click on the style name or Right-click on it and choose **Apply "[name of style]."** This will automatically apply the style—with all of the styling you created— to the entire paragraph in which your cursor is positioned.

How Do I... Create a Basic Object Style?

Object styles are useful for creating non-text elements in your document, such as image and text frames (with strokes and fills), sidebars, or even tables. I am not going to go deep into this rabbit hole because it can go on forever; suffice it to say that this tip is to make you aware of the existence of object styles and tell you where and how to start. Then you can dive into the settings to build up some powerful styles for your objects. I like to format my object in my document first, and then create my style from that, so I can tweak as I go before locking in the style. In the example above, I've created a frame with a dashed, colored stroke and a gradient fill. Once you've created your object, select your frame, click on the panel menu in the upper-right corner of the Object Styles panel **(Window > Styles > Object Styles)**, and select **New Object Style**. This brings up a very powerful settings dialog, but for now, just go ahead and name your object style, and then click OK. This creates an object style with all the attributes you applied to the selected frame. You can also create an object style from scratch, without having to create anything in your document first. With nothing selected in your document, click on the Create New Style icon in the Object Styles panel. This will create a new style called Object Style 1 (or Object Style 2, etc.). Double-click on that style to open the Object Style Options dialog. Set up your style options and click OK. Any new styles you create will appear in the Object Styles panel, ready to be applied at any time.

❓ How Do I... Apply an Object Style?

You'll see a pattern emerging here. To apply your object style, create a shape, frame, or object, and then with it selected, click once on the style name in the Object Styles panel, or Right-click on the style name and select **Apply "[name of style]."** This will automatically apply the style to the selected object. This is why styles are so useful and time-saving! It's worth spending the time at the start of any project to set up your styles and preferences to make your workflow smoother.

?) How Do I... Delete a Style?

If you change your mind about a style—maybe you just don't need it anymore or you want to start over—there are several simple ways to get rid of it. First, you can click once on the style name to highlight it, and then click on the trash can icon in the bottom-right corner of the styles panel; or you can Right-click on the style name in the styles panel and select **Delete Style**; or you can highlight the style name, open the styles panel menu, and choose Delete Style from there.

How Do I... Load Styles from Another Document?

As I mentioned previously, I like to create documents with specific text styles, and then save those styles as actual styles in the relative styles panels. I think I win the "most uses of the word 'styles' in a sentence" award for this tip! Anyway, once I have saved my document with its set styles, I can borrow those styles and apply them in a new document. As an example, we'll load some existing character styles into a new document. (*Note:* You can use the same steps to load any other type of styles; just use whichever panel is relevant to the style type you're importing.) Click on the panel menu icon in the upper-right corner of the Character Styles panel and select **Load Character Styles**. Locate the file that contains the styles you wish to import and click OK. This opens a new dialog where you can decide which styles to import. Click on the checkbox next to each style you want to import, and then click OK. You will now see those styles in your Character Styles panel. Just repeat these steps for any other documents or to import any other styles.

How Do I... Find and Delete Unused Styles?

When you've been working on a large project full of styles, you may find yourself at the end wondering if you used all the styles you created or imported. It's good practice to remove any styles you didn't need, and it's really simple to do so. Just go to the relevant styles panel (I recommend clearing up all your styles panels), open the panel, and choose **Select All Unused**. This will highlight the unused styles, and then you can go ahead and delete them all or just the ones you absolutely don't need. You may want to keep some for future import to another document.

⑦How Do I... Override a Style Manually?

Even if you set up a bunch of styles, there may be the odd time you have to go rogue and make some manual amends just as a one off. To do this, go ahead and select the text and make the changes—choose a different color, increase or decrease the size, change the text weight, etc. The text won't snap back to the original style; it will remain as changed. When that text is selected, the name of the style that had previously been applied to it will have a + next to it in the styles panel. If you actually want that style to be overridden with this change globally, just open the panel menu and select **Redefine Style**—this will update the style and all of the text to which it has been applied.

How Do I... Sort Styles by Name?

Once your styles panel starts to build up, you may want to sort your styles by name so you can find one quickly. Open the panel menu and select **Sort By Name**, and this will put all the styles in alphabetical order. You can still click-and-drag them to reorganize the list if you want.

How Do I... Save Styles in CC Libraries?

You can save your styles in your CC Libraries as you create them. At the bottom of the New Character Style (or New Paragraph Style or New Object Style) dialog, click on the checkbox next to Add to CC Library and open the pop-up menu to select the library in which you want to save the style. You can also select **Create New Library** to set up a brand-new one. CC Libraries are great for making style guideline folders for specific branding projects, as they can contain color swatches, color theme sets, fonts, styles, and even styled objects. As versatile as an egg!

When you copy text from other applications and paste it into your InDesign document, the text can often look like a dog's dinner: atrocious formatting and just a nightmare to go through and repair. But in your InDesign Preferences, under Clipboard Handling, there is an option to allow all style information markers to be imported (or not, in which case all the style formatting is stripped and you can manually change it). To locate this setting, go to **InDesign (PC: Edit) > Preferences > Clipboard Handling** and select **All Information** under When Pasting Text and Tables from Other Applications Paste. Just remember, if the font used in the original document is not available in the InDesign document, the text in question will be highlighted in pink to let you know that you need to find or replace that font in your document.

Chapter 6

How to Work with Color

Swatches, Gradients, Tints, and More!

Color and effects are what graphic designers affectionately know as the super powers to "make it pop" for those requests from clients. I'm joking, we all know it's all about comic sans and WordArt! InDesign isn't all about type and layout, it's got so much more power under the hood. The ability to use color and effects actually saves you from having to jump between apps to create stunning artwork and content. With the Swatches and Color panels you can completely control all the color in your projects, whether it applies to frames, fills, text, strokes, gradients, highlights, or something else. You can create multiple swatches either manually or by extracting colors from placed images (a feature I would love to have in Photoshop), and save them in your CC Libraries (which are covered in chapter 9). It was David Blatner who once said that Photoshop and Illustrator are just plugins for InDesign, and to some extent I would agree with that. InDesign has consistently become a more powerful app for the design professional and has come to celebrate 20 years as the industry standard. I am proud to teach InDesign at conferences such as Photoshop World (don't let the name distract you—it includes design too).

InDesign Fun Fact #6
InDesign CS originally shipped with 78 fonts. Today, with the CC2019 release, it is shipped with 16,000 available fonts and growing.

? How Do I... Select and Create New Colors?

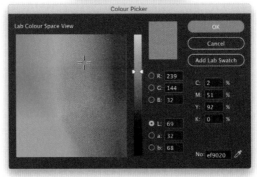

Open the Color panel (go to **Window > Color > Color**—so good they named it twice—or just press **F6**) and double-click on the swatch in the upper-left corner of the panel to open the Color Picker dialog. Wait, before you go to the Color Picker dialog, here's a little trick: Shift-click on the color spectrum bar at the bottom of the Color panel to choose between RGB, CMYK, and Lab. Once you've landed on the color mode you want, open the Color Picker dialog, and that color space will already be chosen. (*Note:* For CMYK, it will still say RGB Color Space View at the top of the dialog, but you'll notice that one of the buttons says Add CMYK Swatch.) Now use one of the following methods to create a new color:

- Click-and-drag the crosshair inside the color field to a new location. The values for the defined color will be shown in the RGB, CMYK, Lab, and Hex fields.
- Drag the slider triangles on either side of the color spectrum up and down to change the tint of the selected color.
- Manually enter values in any of the color value fields (RGB, CMYK, or Lab).

To save the new color as a swatch, click on Add RGB Swatch, Add CMYK Swatch, or Add Lab Swatch in the Color Picker dialog. The button that is available depends on which color value fields are currently selected in the Color Picker dialog (e.g., if you click on one of the RGB fields, you'll see Add RGB Swatch). InDesign then adds the new color to your Swatches panel with the color values as its name. Click OK.

How Do I... Find the Swatches Panel?

The Swatches panel is where the colors for our document live. It's easy enough to find: most panels are located under the Window menu, and this is no exception. Just go to **Window > Color > Swatches** to open the Swatches panel. Once it's open, you can make it float on its own or dock it with any other panels that are already open. The Swatches panel will allow you to assign colors to the stroke and fill of containers (frames and shapes) and text. You can also adjust the tint for each color.

In the Swatches panel, or any panel where you can select a color, there are two swatch icons that represent Fill and Stroke. The Fill icon is the upper-left swatch, and it is a solid square. The Stroke icon is the lower-right swatch, and it looks like an empty frame. The icon that is in front indicates where its color will be applied on the selected object or text (i.e., whether it will be applied to the fill or stroke). Click on the icon in the back to bring it to the front. You can swap the Fill and Stroke colors by clicking on the little reverse icon (double-headed bent arrow). For each, the white box with a diagonal red line means no fill or no stroke. There are a couple of quick ways to apply a fill or stroke to an object. First, simply select the object or text to which you want to apply a color, click on the Fill or Stroke icon, and then click on the swatch you wish to apply. InDesign keeps track of the most recently used solid color, the current fill, or the most recently used gradient, so you can also use a shortcut to quickly apply the last color used to the next object. Just press the comma key, and the most recently used fill or stroke color will be applied to whatever is currently selected in your document. (*Note:* Ensure that the Fill swatch icon is selected before using this shortcut if you're applying a fill; or that the Stroke icon is selected if you're applying a stroke.)

How Do I... Swap My Fill and Stroke Colors in a Snap?

If you've been adjusting a stroke color and then decide you want to swap it with the fill color, you could head over to the Toolbar or Swatches panel and click on the Swap Fill and Stroke icon (the little double-headed arrow above the Fill and Stroke swatches), or you could simply press **Shift-X**. This swaps the colors, or in other words, makes the fill color the stroke color and vise versa. Just pressing **X** will toggle between Stroke and Fill, but it won't swap the colors. Pressing **/** (forward slash) will remove the color value from whichever one is currently selected.

How Do I... Return to the Default Fill and Stroke (No Fill, Black Stroke)?

The default settings for Fill and Stroke in InDesign are no fill and a black stroke. So if you drew a box, it would be empty (no fill) with a thin black stroke around it (usually 1 pt in size). To get back to these default settings, press **D** (you may notice that this is the same key that Photoshop uses for resetting its default Foreground/ Background colors). They say dogs are a man's best friend—well, shortcuts are a designer's best friend!

? How Do I... Make My Swatches Bigger?

If you are old like me, your eyes might prefer that those swatches shown in the Swatches panel were a little larger. If so, there's an easy way to enable this. You can also decide whether you see a list with the swatch names or just thumbnails. All you have to do is open the Swatches panel menu and choose Large List, Small List, Large Thumbnail, or Small Thumbnail. The Small List contains the same information as the Large List; the text is just more compressed. Both lists also show a color mode icon to the far right of each swatch. If you're using one of the thumbnails views, you need to hover over a color swatch to see its color mode.

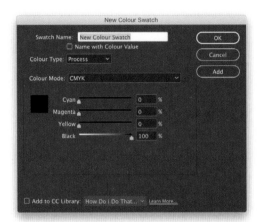

In the Swatches panel, we are often presented with default colors, which include Black, White (paper), Red, Green, and Blue, plus standard CMYK. To add a new color to the panel, open the panel menu and select **New Color Swatch**. In the New Color Swatch dialog, you can play with the sliders to create your own color swatch. Use the Color Mode pop-up menu to choose whether you want to work with CMYK, RGB, or another color mode. To import additional color modes from your computer, select **Other Library** at the very bottom of the pop-up menu and navigate to the file(s) on your system. Give your swatch a name (see the following two tips) and click OK, and your new swatch will appear in the Swatches panel. You'll see throughout this chapter that there are multiple ways to add colors to the Swatches panel from your document, with the Color Picker, with the Color Theme Tool **(Shift-I)**, and more (see pages 138, 150–153, 161, 162, and 164).

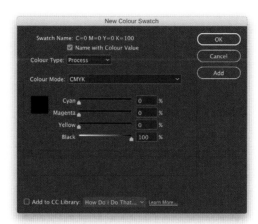

When you create a new color swatch, you have two options for naming it. The first is to name your new swatch with its color value by putting a check mark next to Name with Color Value (this is the default option) in the New Color Swatch dialog. Click OK, and your new swatch will be added to the Swatches panel with its color value as its name. The good thing about this is that you can see the exact color value in the Swatches panel when you're working on your document. But what if you want to give your swatch a descriptive name instead? Next tip, please...

How Do I... Name a Swatch with a Description?

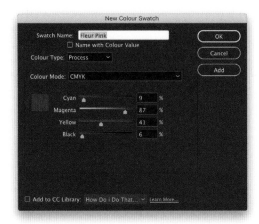

Sometimes the color value of a swatch isn't so important to you, but you want to name it with a very specific description. To do this, uncheck the Name with Color Value option in the New Color Swatch dialog. You can now give your new swatch a name that describes your palette, such as "Sunflower Yellow," or maybe a brand name like "Logo Red." Click OK to add your swatch to the Swatches panel.

⑦ How Do I... Rename a Swatch?

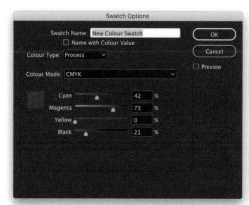 

What if you already have a color value–named swatch and you want to give it a descriptive name instead? Or maybe you have a swatch with a descriptive name and you just want to change it. Double-click on the swatch to open the Swatch Options dialog, and then enter a new name in the Swatch Name field. If your swatch is currently named with its color value, you'll need to uncheck the Name with Color Value option to enable the Swatch Name field. Click OK to save the new name. You can also just click once on the swatch to select it, and then click on its name again to open a text field right in the Swatches panel. Type in a new name and press **Return (PC: Enter)** to save it. It's that simple! That's why I like writing these tips—they don't have to be super complicated; they're just simple tips to keep you working fast.

How Do I... Edit an Existing Swatch?

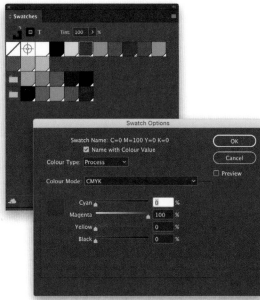

To quickly edit an existing swatch color, go to the Swatches panel and double-click on the swatch icon; Control-click on the selected swatch icon and choose **Swatch Options** from the context menu; or double-click on the little color mode square to the far right of the swatch (in list view only; see note below). In the Swatch Options dialog, you can choose a different color mode, and you can move the sliders to dial in a new color. Click OK, and the changes to your swatch will be saved. There's so much control over color in InDesign. (*Note:* There are two ways to view swatches in the Swatches panel: list view and thumbnail view. Some options are not available in thumbnail view. To select a list view option, open the panel menu and choose Large List or Small List.)

How Do I... Change the Default Swatches?

When you first open InDesign and go to the Swatches panel, you'll have a set of very generic default swatches, but you can create a new set of default swatches to better suit your needs. With no documents open (this is standard practice for setting up any default options for all future documents in that session), go to your Swatches panel and delete the swatches you don't need, or edit them, add new ones, reorder them, rename them—all of these methods are covered in this chapter. These will now be your default swatches for any new documents you open from this point forward (until you set up new defaults).

TIP: SAVE YOUR SWATCHES

One thing to keep in mind is that when you're creating new swatch collections, you should always save them, either by adding them to your CC Libraries (see page 166), or by saving them as an ASE file on your computer or in cloud storage. To save them as an ASE file, simply select the swatch colors in the Swatches panel, open the panel menu, and choose **Save Swatches**. Save the file in your chosen location for future use.

How Do I... Borrow Swatches from Another Document?

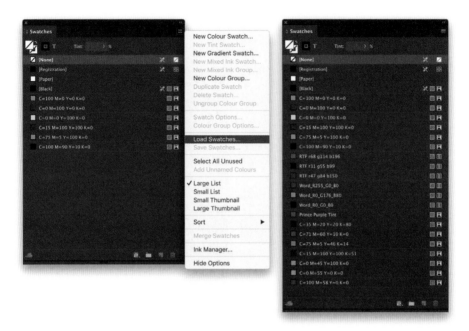

If you've created some custom color swatches in another document, you can borrow those swatches—the whole collection—and import them into your new or current document. Go to your Swatches panel, open the panel menu, and select **Load Swatches**. In the Open a File dialog, navigate to the document that contains the swatches you want to use, and click Open. The swatches from that document will be loaded into the Swatches panel for your currently open document and you can start using them straight away. As always, I recommend saving your swatch collections for future use (see page 149) in case you lose the documents in which they are stored.

How Do I... Save a Color from My Color Panel to My Swatches Panel?

We've covered a LOT of color tips in this chapter, and here's another quicky! If you've created a new color in the Color panel, the fastest way to save that color to your Swatches panel is to just drag-and-drop it. Click-and-hold directly on the preview swatch you created in the Color panel, and then drag it over to the Swatches panel. When your cursor reaches the Swatches panel, you'll see it change to a tiny little hand with a plus (+) sign next to it. You can decide where in the list you want your new swatch to appear by hovering over that location; you'll see a horizontal line appear where your swatch will land when you drop it like it's hot. Just let go of the mouse button (I do apologize to all tablet users; you know what to do), and that new custom color will now be saved as a swatch in your Swatches panel. Told you it was simple!

How Do I... Load Pantone Colors into My Swatches Panel?

If you need to work with Pantone colors in your document, it's not a problem—they are right there in the Swatches panel. Open the panel menu and choose **New Color Swatch**. In the New Color Swatch dialog, click on the Color Mode pop-up menu, and you'll see a list of all the color libraries included with InDesign. Choose the one you need (in this case, PANTONE+ Solid Coated), and that set of colors will be loaded immediately. To choose a particular color from this set—say, Orange 021, a favorite of one of my favorite designer friends, Mr. Aaron Draplin of draplin.com—type the number into the PANTONE field or find your color in the Pantone list and select it. Then click Add, followed by Done (unless you want to select other colors as well; in which case, just select more and click Add each time, before finally clicking Done). The colors you add will appear in the Swatches panel with their Pantone names. To add multiple colors at once, Command-click (PC: Ctrl-click) on the individual Pantone swatches you want to import, and then click the Add button. If you want to import the entire Pantone set into your Swatches panel, click on the first visible Pantone color at the top of the list, then scroll down to the bottom of the list and Shift-click on the last swatch. Click Done, and the full collection of Pantone swatches in that set will be loaded into your Swatches panel. Much like with fonts, you'll spend all your time scrolling through the hundreds of swatches you now have. You can, of course, delete some once you realize you loaded way too many!

How Do I... Add New Colors from My Document to My Swatches Panel?

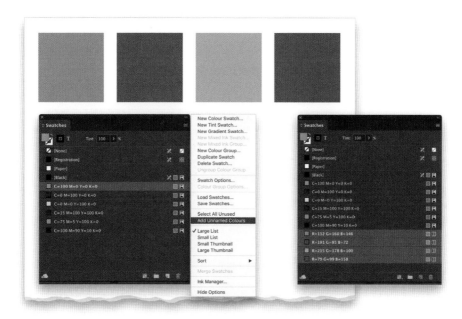

Let's say you started adding some new objects into your document and applied a different color to each object. After a while you may have added a few new colors to your document and then think "dang, I need to add all these to my Swatches panel." Fear not, just open the Swatches panel menu and choose **Unnamed Colors**, and those new colors will automatically be added to your Swatches panel. They will be named with their color values, but you can always rename them.

⑦ How Do I... Organize My Swatches?

Once you start building up some swatches, you'll want to organize them for easier access and management. One of the quickest ways to do this is to organize your colors into groups. Start by going to the Swatches panel and selecting the colors you want to include in the group (click on one color and then Shift-click on another to select those two colors and all colors in between; or Command-click [PC: Control-click] on individual colors to select nonconsecutive colors). Then Right-click on the selected colors and choose **New Color Group**. This will bring up the New Color Group dialog where you can name your color group. Click OK, and your new group will appear in the Swatches panel.

? How Do I... Delete Swatches Quickly?

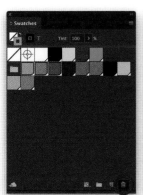 

Sometimes you just want to get down and dirty and delete a bunch of unneeded swatches really quickly, with no regrets! Just go to the Swatches panel and select the swatch or swatches you don't want anymore, and then click on the little trash-can icon at the bottom of the panel. Or you can Right-click on a swatch and select **Delete Swatch**. You will be presented with a dialog that asks you what swatch you would like to use in place of the deleted swatch (or swatches). This ensures that if you've chosen to delete a swatch that has been applied somewhere in your document, the replacement swatch will now be used wherever the original swatch was applied. Make your selection and click OK.

How Do I... Merge Swatches?

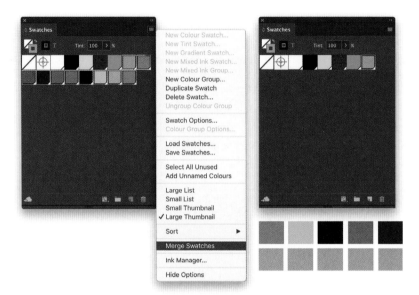

What does "merge swatches" actually mean? It doesn't mean you get a bunch of swatches and merge them all into one big ugly color. Rather, when you merge swatches, you remove a group of swatches (maybe duplicates or swatches that are similar) and replace them with a single color swatch. Here's how it works: Select the swatch you want to keep, and then Shift-click or Command-click (PC: Ctrl-click) on the swatches you want to merge. Now when you Right-click and choose **Merge Swatches**, you will keep the first swatch you selected and remove all the others. The first swatch will replace the others wherever they were used in your document.

How Do I... Find and Delete Unused Swatches?

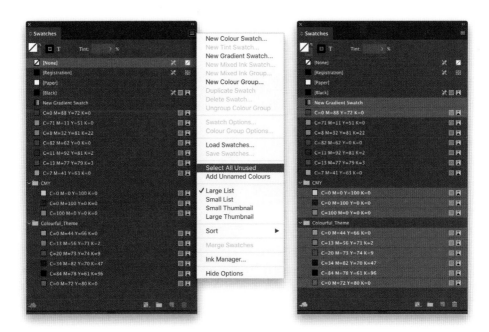

When you've finished creating your new document and you need to share it with another designer, print company, or output service provider, it's good practice to make the document as uncluttered as possible (lose what you don't use!). This helps to prevent any confusion about what should be included in that document, particularly when it comes to color. Ideally, you'll delete any unused color swatches from the Swatches panel so that the other party will know exactly which colors are used in the document. To clean up your Swatches panel, open the panel menu and choose **Select All Unused**. This highlights all of your unused swatches. Now just click on the trash can icon at the bottom of the Swatches panel to delete them all in one go.

? How Do I... Create a Tint of a Color?

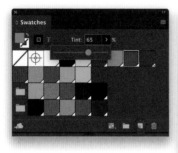

Creating a tint of a color (a percentage of that original color) is super easy. Select the color you want to work with in the Swatches panel, and then click on the arrow to the right of the Tint field at the top of the panel to open a slider. Move the slider from 100% to a lower number to create a tint of the selected color. To avoid losing this tint (as you may want to take the slider back to 100% to use the original color), you have to save it as its own swatch. Once the Tint slider is at the percentage you need, click on the New Swatch icon at the bottom of the Swatches panel, and the new tint will be saved as a totally new and separate color swatch. The catch is that this tint swatch is linked to the original color swatch, so if you change the color of the original swatch, the tint will adjust to that new color as well. And if you delete the original color, the tint will also be deleted. To prevent this from happening, Right-click on your tint swatch and select **New Color Swatch**. Make sure everything looks good in the New Color Swatch dialog and click OK. This will create a new independent swatch with the color values of the tint, which means if you modify or delete the original swatch, this independent tint swatch will not be affected.

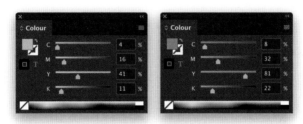

If you've created a new color using the Color panel and you decide you want to try a darker shade of that color, you can do so by adjusting the sliders. For example, with the CMYK sliders, you can drag the K (black) slider to the right to make the color darker, or to the left to make it lighter. For both the RGB and CMYK sliders, there is a little trick you can use to make an even adjustment to the color. All you have to do is press-and-hold the Shift key as you drag a slider to the left or right, and the other sliders will move with it until the one closest to the end hits its maximum. This adjusts the shade of the color evenly. Moving the sliders to the lighter end will lighten the color until it hits white.

How Do I... Pick Up Attributes from My Document with the Eyedropper Tool?

When you double-click on some of the tools in the Toolbar, you will bring up additional settings for those tools. The Eyedropper Tool is one of the tools that has this option, making it a pretty powerful tool. It can pick up a multitude of attributes in your document; not just color. Double-click on the Eyedropper Tool to open the Eyedropper Options dialog. You'll see six different settings groups: Stroke Settings, Fill Settings, Character Settings, Paragraph Settings, Object Settings, and Transform Options. Click on the arrow to the left of each group to examine the attributes that can be collected with the Eyedropper Tool. For example, you can use the Eyedropper to collect Color and Tint—that's a simple one. But say you type some text and you want to pick up the attributes of that text and apply it to other text in your document. First, make sure you have the suitable Character Settings checked in the Eyedropper Options dialog. Then select the Type Tool **(T)** and highlight the text whose settings you want to use. Now select the Eyedropper Tool **(I)** and click on the text you want to change—voila, that text now matches your source text. I suggest you look through all of the settings in the Eyedropper Options dialog and start using that Eyedropper to make some quick changes in your document. The same applies to the Color Theme Tool **(Shift-I)**, which is nested within the Eyedropper Tool flyout in the Toolbar. Double-click on the Color Theme Tool to open its options dialog. Here you can select a preset that decides how colors are captured when you use the Color Theme Tool to select a range of colors from your image.

How Do I... Sample Single Colors Using the Color Picker?

The regular Eyedropper Tool lets you choose colors from any part of an image or anything with color in your document. But an even more powerful tool is the Color Picker Tool from the Color Picker dialog. To get to it, open the Color panel **(Window > Color > Color)** and double-click on the Fill icon (also works with the Stroke). To sample a color with the Color Picker, click-and-hold on the eyedropper icon in the bottom-right corner of the Color Picker dialog (don't release the mouse yet), and drag it over an image, object, or anything else on your computer screen—it doesn't even have to be in the InDesign interface—to pick a color from that item. When you're hovering over the color you want to sample, you will see that color appear under the crosshair in the Color Picker dialog. Now just release your mouse, and your color will be selected. You can see the RGB, CMYK, Lab, and HEX values of this selection in your Color Picker dialog, and all values are still editable.

How Do I... Extract a Color Theme from an Image or Object?

The Color Theme Tool allows you to extract a set of five color swatches from anything that has color in your document. The swatches are based on the colors present in the area you choose as your localized area. Select the Color Theme Tool **(Shift-I)** from the Toolbar and click on any part of an image or artwork in your document to pick a color palette. The tool will retain the five strongest colors in that area, and they will appear in a mini panel. If you switch to another tool, these colors will be held until you go back to the tool. To view other variations of the color palette, click on the arrow to the right of the five swatches in the mini panel. To apply one of the colors, make sure the Color Theme Tool is selected in the Toolbar, click on a single color in the mini panel, and move your cursor over the object or text to which you want to apply the color. The little eyedropper icon is carrying the selected color, and depending on what the tool is hovering over, you'll see a mini stroked box, a full fill box, or a little T, for text. This tells you what the color will be applied to if you click in that location. You can save all of the swatches to your Swatches panel by clicking on the Swatches panel icon (looks like a grid with a + sign) in the mini panel. To add only a single color, press-and-hold the Option (PC: Alt) key, click on the color you want to add, and click on the Swatches panel icon. The colors are added to the Swatches panel in a newly created folder. You can also add these colors to your CC Libraries by clicking on the little cloud icon in the mini panel.

How Do I... Make a New Gradient?

Open the Swatches and Gradient panels, and position them next to each other. You can open the Gradient panel by going to **Window > Color > Gradient**, or by double-clicking on the Gradient Swatch Tool in the Toolbar. From the Type pop-up menu, select **Linear** or **Radial**. A linear gradient moves across the object, from one side to the other. A radial gradient starts at the center of the object and goes from dark to light, or vice versa. The default gradient is black to white (you may also see the last gradient you created), but you can choose whichever colors you'd like. To do this easily, click on the gradient swatch in the Gradient panel to activate the color stops beneath the gradient bar at the bottom of the panel. Then just click-and-drag the first color of your choice from the Swatches panel onto one of the color stops in the Gradient panel. When you are ready to drop the color, you will see a small + sign letting you know you are replacing the color. If you don't see that, it means you are adding the new color to the existing ones. Do the same for your second color. (*Note:* You can add more than two colors to the gradient bar when you become more confident with gradients.) You can now slide the color stops along the gradient bar to change the impact of the gradient. You can also click the Reverse icon to switch the colors around. To apply your new gradient, go to the next tip.

? How Do I... Apply a New Gradient to an Object?

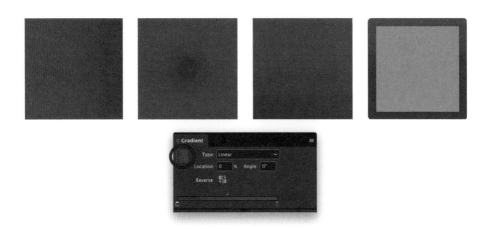

Once you've made your new gradient in the previous tip, you can apply it to an object quite simply. Select your object, select Fill or Stroke (depending on where you want the gradient to be applied) in the Toolbar, and click on the gradient swatch in the Gradient panel. Want to use this gradient again? Add it to your Swatches panel by Right-clicking on the swatch in the Gradient panel and choosing **Add to Swatches**, or by dragging the swatch from the Gradient panel into the Swatches panel. Once it's in the Swatches panel, you can give it a name by clicking on it once to select it, and then clicking on it again to enable the name field.

TIP: USE A KEYBOARD SHORTCUT TO APPLY A GRADIENT

We just applied a gradient to an object. Now let's apply that same gradient to another object by selecting the new object, choosing Fill or Stroke from the Toolbar, and pressing the period (**.**) key. This applies the gradient currently set in the Gradient panel to the selected object.

How Do I... Apply a Gradient Across Multiple Objects?

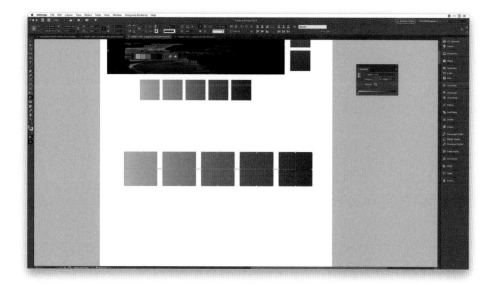

First, ensure that a gradient has already been applied to all selected objects. Then go to the Toolbar and select the Fill or Stroke box (depending on whether you want to apply the gradient to the fill, the stroke, or even both). Select the Gradient Swatch Tool **(G)** and position it where you want to define the beginning point of the gradient. Now click-and-drag across the objects in the direction you want the gradient to be applied. You can press-and-hold the Shift key as you drag to constrain the gradient to multiples of 45°, so that you can apply the gradient across your shapes instead of just in a horizontal or vertical plane. Release the mouse button at the place where you want to define the endpoint of your gradient. This applies the gradient across the collection of objects as though it is a single object. You can now change the gradient settings and it will affect the applied gradient. If you want each shape to hold its individual gradient, but you want to be able to make changes globally, just make copies of the original shape, which will keep the characteristics of the first, and when you make any change to the gradient in use, it will be applied globally to each individual shape.

How Do I... Save Colors to CC Libraries?

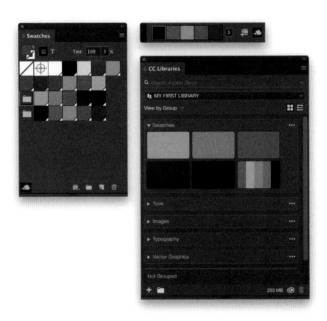

We have seen a couple of color panels now that give us the ability to add swatches to Libraries. You can access and use any items saved to CC Libraries in other documents and Adobe apps. CC Libraries are covered in chapter 10, but seeing as you are here, we'll take a very brief look at how to save color swatches to a library. Open the CC Libraries panel **(Window > CC Libraries)** and select the library to which you want to add your swatches from the pop-up menu near the top of the panel (below the Search field). To create a dedicated swatch library, select **+ Create New Library** at the bottom of that pop-up menu, give your library a name, and click Create. Now, using either the Swatches panel or the Color Theme Picker, just select the colors you want to add to your library, and then click on the little cloud icon with the arrow (if you hover over it, you should see "Add selected swatch to my current CC Library"). That's it! The beauty of building a swatch library is that when you're working remotely or in another Adobe app and you need to get ahold of some specific swatches, you can access them quickly and easily in the CC Libraries panel. Like I mentioned, you'll find out more about how to use CC Libraries in chapter 10.

How Do I... Find Hex Code for Colors?

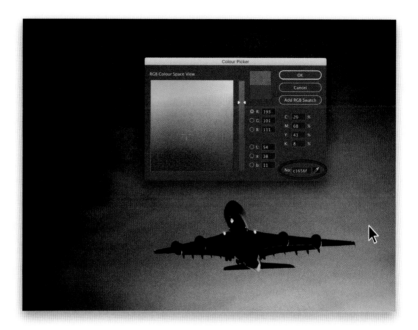

To find and select a hexadecimal color code, open the Color Picker dialog (click on the Fill icon in the Toolbar, Color panel, or Control panel) and make sure the RGB fields are selected. Now, click-and-hold on the eyedropper tool in the bottom-right corner of the dialog, and drag it over any area on the screen. The hex color value from that area will be displayed in the field next to the eyedropper in the Color Picker dialog. When you're satisfied with your selection, release your mouse. Click on Add RGB Swatch to add the color swatch to your Swatches panel. Previously, the hex value edit field was available only in the Color Picker dialog and the New Color Swatch dialog in RGB color mode. In CC2018 and all subsequent versions, however, the hex value edit field is also available in the Color panel when the RGB sliders are displayed. This is so useful when you want to view or add hex values in your document.

What Is a hex code? Without going deep into its complete meaning, you will recognize hex codes if you're working with web graphics. You'll often see a color value of, say, #000000 for black and #ffffff for white. You can find more information on hex values on the internet.

Chapter 7

How to Work with Images and Graphics

Become a Graphics Master

They say a picture paints a thousand words, and it can also be said that in InDesign, you can still add a thousand words when using images! Because that's what InDesign is for! Of course, you can make a document with only images if you want to. One important thing to know about images in InDesign is that you can build documents with images that are linked from source files, or you can embed them into the document. I use linked images 99 percent of the time. This means that the original image file is stored in a location outside of InDesign, and when you "place" the image in your document, you create a link to that original file. If you break the link by moving the original file, you get a warning, and if you make changes to the original, you get a warning. InDesign is great at telling you when something is wrong. When you embed images in your InDesign document, you increase the file size of the document, but everything stays together. In this chapter, we'll look at how to place images, check links, resize and adjust images, check image resolution, and set image preferences. You can also add cool special effects without having to jump over to Photoshop (but it's really easy to do that from InDesign if you need to). We'll look at how to add images into text, use blend modes to create effects, and use images to reflow text in a document. Then there's how to use CC Libraries to manage your images, how to work with Adobe Bridge, and a bunch of other tips and tricks. Because InDesign works so seamlessly with Photoshop, Illustrator, and the Creative Cloud, it's not difficult to make something incredible. Just pick up any photo book and see how beautiful and well laid out it is—this is what InDesign brings to you in terms of design capability!

InDesign Fun Fact #7

InDesign is the successor to PageMaker, which was acquired by Adobe when they purchased Aldus in 1994. I was almost 30 in 1994. I feel very old now, as I used PageMaker back in the olden days!

How Do I... Decide What File Type to Use for My Graphics?

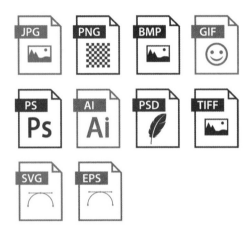

InDesign is pretty flexible when it comes to the file formats that can be placed into a document. The obvious ones are a given: AI, EPS, PDF, and PSD. InDesign also accepts TIFF, JPG, and PNG. You can easily replace each format with any other format, and you can even edit any of them outside of InDesign and have them update in your document (see page 177).

(?) How Do I... Place an Image?

There are a few ways to place an image. We'll run through the menu option first. You can start by creating a frame on the page to place an image into, but if you skip that step and go straight to placing the image, a frame is automatically created for it—InDesign is clever like that! With your document open, go to **File > Place** (or **File > Place from CC Libraries**) and select your chosen graphic or image (photo). Once you click Open, you'll see a small thumbnail of the image floating with your cursor. Now just click-and-drag from your starting point outward until you reach the image size you want, and then release. Don't worry if you get a little trigger-happy and click once on the document and your image is placed at full size. You can easily resize it by pressing-and-holding **Command-Shift (PC: Ctrl-Shift)** while dragging a corner of the frame inward or outward. This will resize both the image and the frame. Another way to place an image is to drag it from a folder onto your document. Just like before, you'll have a little floating thumbnail with your cursor, and you can click-and-drag to place the Image at whatever size you wish. You can also copy and paste an image into your document, but I do not recommended this method because when you do so, the original image file will not be linked to the document and you can run into issues further down the line.

? How Do I... Resize an Image?

All images in InDesign are enclosed within a frame. This frame determines how much of the image you can see, so when you resize the frame you'll notice that the image isn't resized with it. To resize both the frame and the image, press-and-hold **Command-Shift (PC: Ctrl-Shift)** as you click-and-drag a corner point of the frame inward or outward. (The Shift key constrains the image while the Command [PC: Ctrl] key ensures that the frame and image are resized proportionally.) If you want to resize from the center, you also need to hold down the Option (PC: Alt) key. So to resize a frame and image proportionally from the center outward, you need to press-and-hold **Command-Option-Shift (PC: Ctrl-Alt-Shift)** as you click-and-drag from the center point. Think of it as a finger workout!

TIP: PREVIEW THE IMAGE AS YOU RESIZE IT
When you use the method described above, you won't see the image resize until you release your mouse (you'll only see the frame resize). However, if you want to see a live preview of the image as you resize it, just hold down your click for an extra couple of seconds before you start dragging. This is called the "Patient User Mode" — Terry White and Scott Kelby taught me that!

How Do I... Fit My Image to My Frame (or Vice Versa)?

InDesign's Frame Fitting controls allow you to manually fit your content to its frame, or fit your frame to the content within it. To apply a Frame Fitting option, select the frame, and then go to **Object > Fitting** and select one of the options, or click on one of the Frame Fitting icons in the Properties panel or Control panel. Keep in mind that you always have the option to adjust the content or frame after the fact—these options are to help you get there quickly. The following options are available:

Fill Frame Proportionally: The image will fit in the frame as best as possible, with some areas of the image falling outside of the frame. The frame will be filled.

Fit Content Proportionally: The entire image will appear within the frame, but there will be white space if the image and frame do not have the same aspect ratio.

Fit Content to Frame: This will stretch the image to fill the entire frame. The image is not resized proportionally and can look awful.

Fit Frame to Content: The frame is resized to fit the content. If the placed image is bigger than the document the image will suddenly fill the page. This option is useful only if the image is smaller than the document into which it's being placed.

Center Content: This shows the center section of the image at whatever size the frame is, unless the image fits the frame perfectly when placed.

Content-Aware Fit: The image fills the frame and is placed with what InDesign deems to be the optimum part of the image showing (see next tip).

How Do I... Use Content-Aware Fit to Fit an Image into a Frame?

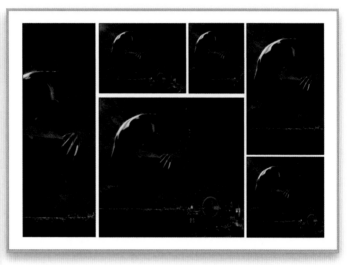

Content-Aware Fit attempts to automatically and intelligently fit the optimum part of an image inside a frame. This is assuming you don't want the whole image showing in the frame, just a cropped version. Now, what InDesign thinks is "the best part of an image" is subject to question—it is just AI (Adobe Sensei) trying its best to work it out. I use Content-Aware Fit to help me find a better starting point. This feature is not enabled by default. If you want it to be the default option so that it is automatically applied to all placed images, then go to **InDesign CC (PC: Edit) > Preferences > General** and put a check mark next to "Make Content-Aware Fit the default frame-fitting option" (at the bottom of the dialog). You can also apply it to individual image frames by selecting an image frame and going to **Object > Fitting > Content-Aware Fit**, or by clicking on the Content-Aware Fit icon in the Properties panel. As I said, this is more of a "try it and see" kind of approach. If you find it works, then leave it on; you can always adjust the image placement afterward. This feature seems to work better with photographs than with logos or images created as vector graphics in Illustrator. In the example above, I've placed the same image into six frames of different sizes and shapes. You can see that the image is positioned differently in each frame so that the primary content (the figure) is the focal point of the image. You can still reposition the image manually after you've used Content-Aware Fit (see the tip on the next page).

?How Do I... Reposition an Image in a Frame?

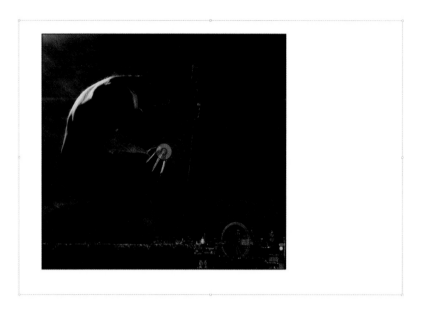

Even after you have used one of the Frame Fitting options, you may want to reposition your image within the frame. Choose the Selection Tool **(V)** and then double-click on the image, or click on the little donut in the center of the image, and you can manually drag the image around the frame. Use the arrow keys to make smaller adjustments. You'll see a frame that shows the boundaries around the actual full image as you move it.

How Do I... Preview My Image While Moving it Around Within a Frame?

I briefly covered this in another tip, but I wanted to put it into its own tip because it can be very helpful when you're positioning images in InDesign. This is called "Patient User Mode" by Scott Kelby and Terry White. When you place an image into a frame and it is much larger than the frame, you can use the Direct Selection Tool (**A**) to click on the little donut in the center of the image and drag it around in the frame. The only problem is you don't see a live preview of where you're moving the image. However, if you click-and-hold on the image for two seconds before you start to move it, you will be able to see the entire image as you move it. The portion of the image that is outside the frame will be ghosted, and the part that is within the frame is not ghosted.

? How Do I... Edit an Image After it's Been Placed?

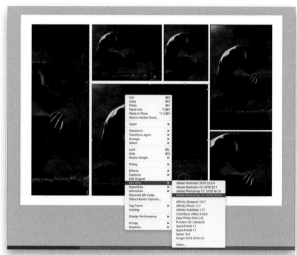 

Let's say you've placed an image or graphic into your document and you decide that the image needs an edit or tweak. The beauty of InDesign is that when you place an image, you're actually creating a link to the original image file. If you want to edit the image, just click on the image frame to select it, then Right-click and choose **Edit With**. You'll be presented with a second list of all the software applications installed on your machine. Select the application you want to use—say, Photoshop—and the image will be opened in that application. Make your edits and save the file. When you come back to InDesign the edits are automatically applied to the image.

TIP: KEEP AN EYE ON YOUR LINKS PANEL

Make sure you check your Links panel regularly; sometimes if an image is edited outside of InDesign and it's in one of your documents, you'll get a warning in the Links panel notifying you that it's been modified.

?) How Do I... Place Multiple Images?

InDesign also allows you to place multiple images at once. Now, when I say this, what I mean is that InDesign allows you to load your cursor, or "place gun," with multiple images, and then release them one-by-one. Think of it like drawing out multiple frames on a page, one after the other. Let's place a series of six random images onto a page. Go to **File > Place** and select six images from the same folder, and then click Open. (It pays to create documents in an orderly fashion, so I recommend organizing all your assets for each document into prepared folders.) When you come back to the document, your place gun is loaded with the images you selected, in the order in which you selected them, but you don't actually have to place them in that order. Press the left and right arrow keys to scroll through the selection of images. You will see a tiny thumbnail of each image as you scroll, so it's easy to select the next image to place. Just click-and-drag in your document to place each image. You can release each one at whatever size you see fit. In the upper-left corner of the visible thumbnail, you'll see the number of images that still need to be placed.

How Do I... Place Images in a Grid?

This is a great shortcut for placing images on a page in a grid-style layout. First, to make life easier for you, make sure all of your images are in the same folder. And for the best effect, choose all portrait-oriented or all landscape-oriented images. Go to **File > Place**, select all of the images you want to place in a grid, and click Open. You'll see the little image place gun, and if you press-and-hold **Command-Shift (PC: Ctrl-Shift)**, you'll see the image thumbnail change to a small grid. While holding down these keys, drag your cursor across the page, and when you release the mouse button, your images will be laid out in an equally spaced grid. Depending on the size of the grid frames you dragged out, the images may not fill the frames completely. In this case, just click on the Fill Frame Proportionally icon in the Control panel, and all the selected frames will be filled. This is a really cool trick for making contact sheets.

How Do I... Make a Triptych?

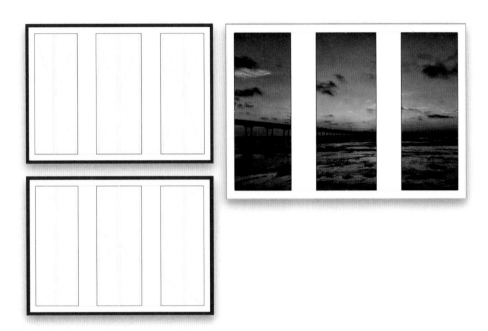

This tip is really useful when you want one image to fit into multiple shapes without requiring you to place multiple versions of the same image in each shape. Start by creating your first frame or shape. Then switch to the Direct Selection Tool **(A)**, press-and-hold the **Option (PC: Alt) key**, and click-and-drag to create a duplicate shape. Release your shape, and then repeat the steps once more to create a triptych-style layout. Now if you were to select all the shapes with the Direct Selection Tool and try to **File > Place** an image, the image would be placed only into whichever shape you click on. To enable the image to span all three shapes, you need to combine the shapes. With all the shapes selected, you can either go to **Object > Paths > Make Compound Path** or press **Command-8 (PC: Ctrl-8)** to convert the three shapes into one frame. Now when you go to **File > Place** and select your image, it drops into the three shapes as one image. This means you can move the image around until you're satisfied with its placement. But what if you want to move one of the shapes? Okay, a couple of steps will rectify this. Select the shapes again and go to **Object > Paths > Release Compound Path**. This releases the shapes and the image will appear only in the first shape in which you placed it. Now move the shapes into a different position or resize them, select them all, and hit **Command-8 (PC: Ctrl-8)**. Voila, the image fills all the shapes again.

? How Do I... Place an Image via Adobe Bridge?

In addition to using CC Libraries, we can also use good old Adobe Bridge to add images to our InDesign documents. I like Bridge and I use it all the time if I am working on a project that includes multiple images. Just get Bridge up and running, select the image (or images) you want to place into your InDesign document, Right-click on it, and select **Place > In InDesign**. This will take you back into InDesign, where you'll have a loaded place gun ready for you so you can place your image(s). If you already had a frame selected in your document, the image will automatically place itself into that frame—it's a little gotcha you have to watch for!

How Do I... Place PSD Layers into a Document?

When placing a layered PSD file into your document, you can make it so that only specific layers are visible. Go to **File > Place**, select your layered PSD file, and put a check mark next to Show Import Options near the bottom of the Place dialog. When you click Open, you will be presented with the Image Import Options dialog. Click on the Layers tab at the top of the dialog and make sure the Show Preview checkbox is selected so you can see a small preview of the image. Under Show Layers, you will see all of the layers in the file. Click on the little eye icon to the left of a layer to hide that layer; click once more in that same spot to unhide it. In the example above right, you can see that I've hidden the background layer. Once you've hidden the layers you don't want to use, click OK, and only the visible layers will be placed into your document.

The Links panel is one of the most important panels in InDesign. This not only lists all the assets in your document, but it also warns you of any problems, such as when you have missing links or images that have been edited outside of InDesign and need to be updated. (*Note:* See the next tip for information about how to repair a missing link.) The Links panel also displays a lot of important information for each asset, such as file name, file type, resolution, color space, size, and metadata. If there's anything wrong with an image or placed asset, just check your Links panel for information.

?How Do I... Repair a Missing Link?

If any of the image files that are linked to your document are moved from their original folder to a new location, the link between the document and the image is broken. When this happens, InDesign will tell you that something is wrong by displaying a red "?" icon on the offending image. If you open up the Links panel **(Window > Links)**, the list of images in your current document will be displayed and the image with the broken link will have the same symbol. Click on the image filename to select it, and in the details panel below the list of images, you'll see the Link Info for that image. The Status will be Missing. To relink this image, Right-click on the filename in the Links panel, choose **Relink**, and select the image from its new location. Another option is to find the image in its current location on your computer and move it back to its original location. This will fix the issue and InDesign will be happy again because the image is linked to its original home.

DICKIE PELHAM

If you have an image placed in a document and want to find out where the source file for that image lives, Right-click on the image and select **Graphics**. This will open a flyout menu with three options: Reveal in Finder (PC: Reveal in Windows Explorer), Reveal in Bridge, or Image Color Settings.

? How Do I... Hide and Reveal Images?

Sometimes you'll want to quickly hide an image in a document, maybe so you can see something behind it. To do this, select the image and press **Command-3 (PC: Ctrl-3)** to hide the frame and image. Press **Command-Option-3 (PC: Ctrl-Alt-3)** to bring them both back. If you want to keep the frame live, but hide the image, it's just one more step. Double-click on the image inside the frame and press **Command-3 (PC: Ctrl-3)**, and the image vanishes, but the frame remains. Press **Command-Option-3 (PC: Ctrl-Alt-3)** to bring the image back.

How Do I... Adjust the View Resolution of My Document?

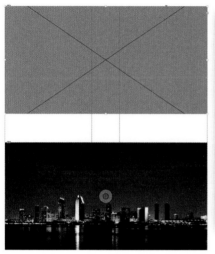

When you're placing images in InDesign, your document may start to fill up with lots of high-resolution images, and that can slow things down somewhat. To make things run a little more smoothly, you can ask InDesign to show low-res versions of the images, or no images at all, while you build your document. This option can be turned on and off manually for each individual image in your document, or it can be set as a default preference for all images. To select this option manually, Right-click on an image, select **Display Performance**, and choose **Fast Display, Typical Display**, or **High Quality Display**. Fast Display will show only an image placeholder, which has a gray fill and a large X indicating an image is present. The donut will also be visible, and you can still resize the image while in Fast Display, but there's not much point when you can't see it. Typical Display will show a low-res version of the image, and High Quality Display will show a high-res version of the image. To set a default display quality for all images, press **Command-K (PC: Ctrl-K)** to open the Preferences dialog, and then click on Display Performance In the column on the left. Select your preferred setting from the Default View pop-up menu near the top of the dialog and click OK. All future placed images will use this display quality setting.

187

? How Do I... Check Image Resolution for Printing?

There's one thing a lot of people miss when creating documents with images: image resolution. More often than not, the document will be printed, and therefore it's best if the images are placed at a minimum of 300PPI. But we don't always get high-res images, and if we don't check, we won't know...until InDesign tells us! Once you've placed an image, you can go to the Info panel or the Links panel to see the Actual PPI and Effective PPI settings for the selected image. A low-res image can be used if its size is reduced because its effective PPI will increase. Let's look at a basic example. If you place a 300PPI image at its fullest, actual size, its effective PPI will be 300PPI. If you shrink that image, its effective PPI becomes larger because there is now more information in a smaller frame. If you make the image larger than its full size, you'll see a decrease in the effective PPI, but you can still get away with printing down to 240PPI. If you place a low-res 72PPI image at full size, it's already too low, and if you enlarge it, it's even worse. But if you make it a lot smaller, you may be able to get its effective PPI up close to 300PPI; it just depends on how big you need the image to be in the document. ALWAYS go back to where the original image came from and either request a high-res file or explain that the image is low-res and can't be used at full size.

How Do I... Manage Images Using Creative Cloud (CC) Libraries?

CC Libraries are a great way to manage your image assets. Anything saved in CC Libraries is available in all of your Adobe Creative Cloud applications. Go to **Window > CC Libraries** to open the CC Libraries panel. If you've already used CC Libraries, you will see the current library displayed in the panel. If you haven't used this feature yet, you can go ahead and create a new library by either clicking on the pop-up libraries menu near the top of the panel (just below the Search field) and selecting **Create New Library**, or clicking on the panel menu in the top-right corner and selecting **Create New Library** from there. Give your new library a name, and then click Create. Now you can bring in images in a couple of ways. The easiest option is to open the folder where your images are currently stored on your computer, and then drag-and-drop each image file onto the CC Libraries panel. The image files will then begin syncing with your library (this may take a little time, depending on your internet connection). The second method is covered in the next tip. You can create as many libraries as you'd like, and call on them by selecting each one from the pop-up menu near the top of panel. To use an image stored in a library, just click-and-drag it from the CC Libraries panel onto your document, and it will behave as though you have used **File > Place**. You can select and place multiple images at once, but for some strange reason, the "place as grid" tip doesn't work in this case.

How Do I... Add an Image from My Document to a CC Library?

If you want to add an image from your document to a CC Library, just create a new library (or open an existing one), select the image in your document you wish to add, and then click on the little + sign in the bottom-left corner of the CC Libraries panel. You'll see a box with the word Graphic appear above that + sign—this is the library acknowledging that you want to add an image to it. Click on the word Graphic, and the selected image will automatically be added to that library. If you select and add more than one image at a time, they will be added to the library as a grouped set, and you will see multiple images in the icon when added. Only add images as a grouped set if you plan to place those items as a group in the future. To add images to the library as separate, individual images, be sure to select and add each image one at a time.

? How Do I... Add Special Effects to Images?

You can use the Effects panel **(Window > Effects)** to apply a number of different special effects to your images, including things like Drop Shadows, Outer and Inner Glow, and Bevel and Emboss. Open the Effects panel menu, select **Effects**, and choose the effect you'd like to apply to your image. You'll be presented with the Effects dialog, where you can adjust the effect to your liking. (You can also access the Effects dialog by double-clicking on Object in the Effects panel.) Notice that all of the available effects are listed on the left side of the dialog. You can stack multiple effects by putting a check mark next to each effect you'd like to apply. Click on the name of an effect to adjust its settings. Put a check mark next to Preview in the lower-left corner of the dialog to see the results of each effect as it is applied to your image. In the example above, I chose to apply the Outer Glow and Bevel and Emboss effects to the word DESIGN.

How Do I... Blend Text Over a Photo? (Hint: Blend Modes)

If you use blend modes in Photoshop, you'll love InDesign's Effects panel **(Window > Effects)**. In the pop-up menu in the top-left corner of the panel, you'll find most of the same blend modes that are available in Photoshop. This is especially useful if you'd like to blend text over a photo. Simply position your text over your image, select the text frame, and then go to the Effects panel and choose a blend mode from the pop-up menu—that's it! You can adjust the opacity before or after applying the blend mode by opening the Opacity pop-up menu near the top-right corner of the panel and adjusting the slider. Not only that, but once you have applied a blend mode, you can still add an additional effect by opening the panel menu, selecting Effects, and choosing an appropriate effect. The example above has four versions of the word "DESIGN," each with a different blend mode applied to show how it reacts with the image below. The blend modes shown are as follows (from top to bottom): Multiply, Overlay, Color Dodge, and Color. You can play around with different blend modes to get the best effect depending on the color of your text and the image you've used.

(For this example, I used the font DDC Hardware available from https://www.font seed.com/fonts/ddc-hardware. Personal and commercial licenses are available. DDC Hardware is dedicated to Aaron's dad, James Patrick Draplin, 1943–2013.)

How Do I... Fill Text with an Image (Part 1)?

In this example, once you fill your text with an image, the text will no longer be editable, so you'll need to start by making sure that your type is set and sized correctly on the page. (For this example, I'm using the word "CAMERA" in ITC Avant Garde Gothic Pro from Typekit.) Now click on the text frame with the Selection Tool **(V)**, and go to **Type > Create Outlines**, which converts the letters into shapes. To place your image into the text, select the text frame once more, go to **File > Place**, choose your image, and click Open. If you want to reposition the image within the text, just double-click anywhere on the image to select it. You can then move the image with the arrow keys on your keyboard or with your cursor. When you're satisfied with the result, just click outside the frame. Because this is now a bunch of shapes, you can distort the text by selecting different points on each letter with the Direct Selection Tool **(A)**, and then dragging them out or using the arrow keys to adjust the lengths. You can also add a stroke to the text, even though you can't edit it.

This tip allows you to fill text with an image and keep the text live so it's still editable. We need two images to do this, one for the background and one for the text. For the text I'm using a Photoshop transparency grid pattern (Image 1), and for the background I'm using a photocopy texture (Image 2). Start by placing Image 1 into your document, and then create another frame that completely covers Image 1, and place Image 2 in this frame. Make sure it completely covers the underlying image; it's the only way this particular technique works. We'll use a blend mode trick to punch the text-shape through the photocopy texture image, which will make it look like the letters are made from underneath the image. For the text, create a new text frame with no stroke or fill on top of Image 2, then add text. Use a large, bold font to allow the texture through so it's visible, and fill the text with white. Now select the text frame and go to the Effects panel **(Window > Effects)**. Make sure Object is selected and choose **Multiply** from the blend mode pop-up menu. This makes the text vanish, but don't worry, it's still there. Next, go to the Layers panel, select the text layer and Image 2 (do not select Image 1), and group them by selecting **Object > Group**. You'll see a dotted-line frame indicating a grouped set of items. With the new group selected, go back to the Effects panel, make sure Group is selected, and put a check mark next to Knockout Group. This reveals Image 1 through the letter shapes. You can resize the type, but be aware of the text boundary and the underlying image size.

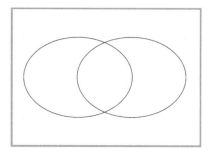

Start by creating two shapes and overlapping them. Then select both shapes and go to **Object > Paths > Make Compound Path** or press **Command-8 (PC: Ctrl-8)**. Go to **File > Place** and select an image to be placed within the two shapes. You'll see that the overlap area is now blank and the other areas are filled with the image. You can now place some text in the blank area, and you are still able to move the image around in the other areas of the frames. Try this with different shapes to create a cool design effect.

FIELD NOTES EDITIONS

FNC-43: SUMMER 2019	NATIONAL PARKS	60,000 PACKS
FNC-42: SPRING 2019	MILE MARKER	35,000 PACKS
FNC-41: WINTER 2018	CLANDESTINE	37,500 PACKS
FNC-40: FALL 2018	END PAPERS	32,000 PACKS
FNC-39: SUMMER 2018	THREE MISSIONS	EDITION SIZE: 50,000 PACKS
FNC-38: SPRING 2018	COASTAL	35,000 PACKS
FNC-37: WINTER 2017	RESOLUTION	35,000 PACKS
FNC-36: FALL 2017	DIME NOVEL	27,500 PACKS
FNC-35: SUMMER 2017	CAMPFIRE	30,000 PACK

Chapter 8

How to Customize Tables

Make Your Data Look Professional

There are multiple ways to access the various table options discussed in this chapter, so I will focus on the methods, menus, and panels that I use most frequently. One of the many benefits of creating tables in InDesign is that you can style your content in so many different ways. Who would have thought you'd ever be making tables that look so flash after using a program like Excel for so long? Yep, I just said Excel when referring to nice-looking tables. Joking aside, InDesign works amazingly with tables, and it allows you to import data from both Excel and Apple's Numbers app. Basically, any table data you need in an InDesign document can be imported and styled. In this chapter, we'll go through some basic and important tips to help you create the best table data possible. Trust me, there are people out there who are impressed by this! Tables and InDesign are important in the real world when it comes to informative design. Just go into a fast food restaurant, eat in, and grab a tray. More often than not, the tray has a sheet of paper with a fun-looking graphic advertising the latest toy or in-store offer. If I had designed that I would be proud of my work. Now flip that sheet over and check out the back. Any good restaurant will have a massive table of food data, ingredients, calorie data, etc., for every item they sell. This is where InDesign and tables come together: the front might be the sales pitch, but that chart on the back is an important element that has to be available. And you still get paid for that kind of work! Tips included in this chapter range from something as simple as how to build your first table to how to place Excel files; add graphics to cells; create header rows; rotate text; merge cells; use fills, strokes, and shading; and quickly add more rows and columns. It's the more technical side of creating in InDesign, but don't underestimate what you can achieve with some basic principles.

InDesign Fun Fact #9

InDesign was the first MAC OSX–native desktop-publishing software.

How Do I... Create a Table?

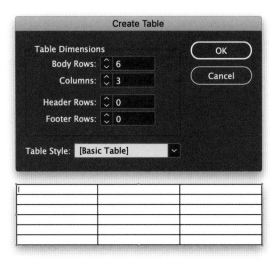

We all love a good table! In fact, there's a whole menu in InDesign just for tables. To quickly place a basic table with default styling into your document, go to **Table > Insert Table.** You'll be presented with a dialog where you can choose the number of columns and rows you'd like your table to have, and whether you want to include any header or footer rows. You also have the opportunity to apply any table styles. (*Note:* See "How Do I Create a Basic Table Style" for information about table styles.) Click OK, and your cursor will be loaded with the table. Now simply click anywhere in your document to place the table. Once it has been placed, you can resize it by clicking-and-dragging any of the points on its frame inward or outward. Your default font will be used when you begin to type into the table.

TIP: A TABLE WITHIN A TABLE

You can even create a table in a cell in a table—table inception! Just click inside a cell and then go to **Table > Insert Table**, choose your dimensions, and click OK.

How Do I... Insert a Table Into a Text Frame?

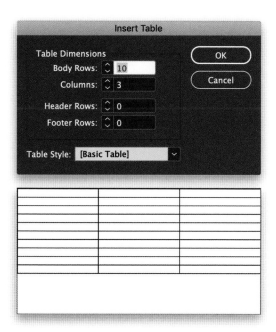

Draw out a text frame on your page, and then go to **Table > Insert Table**. Enter the number of columns and rows you need, choose whether you want any header or footer rows, and click OK. The table will automatically insert itself into the text frame. In the example above I gave my text frame a magenta stroke to make it stand out, and the table has a default black 1 pt stroke, which can be changed after it's been placed.

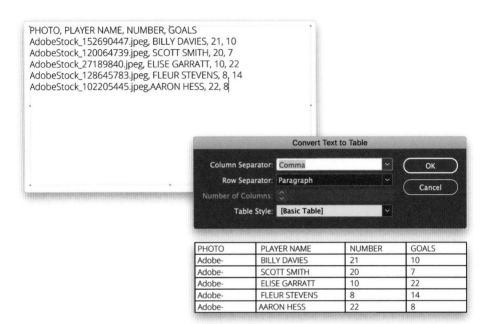

You may already have some text in the form of what is called "tab-delimited text" or "comma-delimited text," often saved as a CSV file type. This is when columns of data are separated by tab characters or commas, and rows of data are separated by paragraph returns. Paste this text into a text frame and then highlight all of the text. Go to **Table > Convert Text to Table** and use the Column Separator menu to specify whether your column data is separated by tabs, commas, or paragraph returns. Next, choose whether your row data is separated by tabs, commas, or paragraph returns. Click OK, and your text will be organized into a basic, unsettled table (unless you want to use a specific table style, which you can select from the dialog before clicking OK; see "How Do I Create a Basic Table Style?" at the end of this chapter). In the example above, my column data was separated by commas, and my row data was separated by paragraph returns.

How Do I... Place an Excel File?

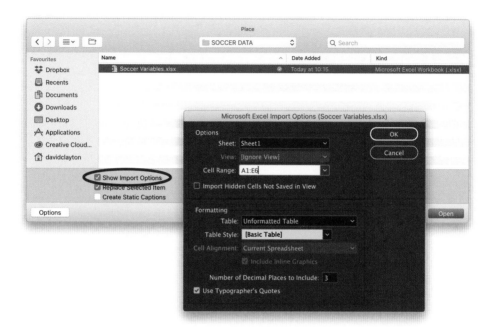

If you have an Excel spreadsheet and you want to turn it into a table in InDesign without having to copy and paste all the data, you can place the Excel file like you would an image. Just go to **File > Place** and locate your file, make sure you have Show Import Options checked, and click OK. This gives you the Microsoft Excel Import Options dialog, where you can select which sheet to import (if your spreadsheet has multiple sheets) and even which cells to import. If you have made any specific formatting adjustments, such as alignments or colored cells, then make sure you select **Formatted Table** from the Table pop-up menu; otherwise, leave this set to the default **Unformatted Table** option to import only the data. Once you've made your selections, click OK. After the table has been placed, you may need to manually adjust some columns to make the data fit, and you can apply any formatting you require.

? How Do I... Select an Entire Table?

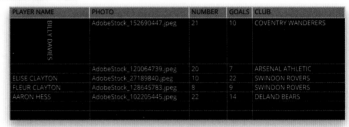

To select an entire table and all its contents with one click, choose the Type Tool **(T)** and move the cursor up to the top-left corner of the table. When you see the cursor change to a 45-degree arrow, click once and all of the table contents, including the table itself, will be selected.

How Do I... Resize Table Columns and Rows?

PHOTO		PLAYER NAME	NUMB
AdobeStock_152690447.jpeg		BILLY DAVID	21
AdobeStock_120064739.jpeg		SCOTT CAMER	20
AdobeStock_27189840.jpeg		ELISE CLAYTON	10
AdobeStock_128645783.jpeg		FLEUR CLAYTO	8
AdobeStock_102205445.jpeg		ALAN HESS	22

Resizing columns and rows in a table is easy if you are doing a quick, manual adjustment. Just hover your cursor over a column or row border and the cursor will change to a double-headed arrow. Then click-and-drag to resize the column to the left of, or the row above, the border you're dragging. You'll only resize one column or row at a time, but don't worry if you want to even things up—there's a tip for that coming up next!

How Do I... Even Up My Columns and Rows?

PLAYER NAME	PHOTO	NUMBER	GOALS	CLUB	CARDS
BILLY DAVIES	Home Kit	21	10	COVENTRY WANDERERS	
SCOTT SMITH	Home Kit	20	7	ARSENAL ATHLETIC	
ELISE CLAYTON	Away Kit	10	22	SWINDON ROVERS	
FLEUR CLAYTON	Home Kit	8	9	SWINDON ROVERS	
AARON HESS	Away Kit	22	14	DELAND BEARS	
ALAN STRANGER	Home Kit	18	12	LOFTUS RANGERS	
PAUL CHUCKLE	Away Kit	14	6	LOFTUS RANGERS	

If you've started to lay out your table and you find that some of your columns or rows need evening out (I tend to find that the rows are the ones I want evened up because my columns are usually set to the widths required for the content) all you need to do is highlight all your rows (and columns by default) and go to **Table > Distribute Rows Evenly**. This will take the average of all the row heights and make all rows the same height. You can still make changes to these heights after the fact.

How Do I... Add Graphics to Table Cells?

PLAYER NAME	PHOTO	NUMBER	GOALS	CLUB	CARDS
BILLY DAVIES	Home Kit	21	10	COVENTRY WANDERERS	
SCOTT SMITH	Home Kit	20	7	ARSENAL ATHLETIC	
	Away Kit	10	22	SWINDON ROVERS	
FLEUR CLAYTON	Home Kit	8	9	SWINDON ROVERS	
AARON HESS	Away Kit	22	14	DELAND BEARS	
ALAN STRANGER	Home Kit	18	12	LOFTUS RANGERS	
PAUL CHUCKLE	Away Kit	14	6	LOFTUS RANGERS	

Back in the old days we had to place an image over a table, but it's actually really easy to place an image into a cell now. Start by resizing the cell to ensure that it can accommodate the image; otherwise, the image will only show partially in the cell. (See page 203 for information on how to resize a cell.) Make sure the cell into which you want to place your image is selected, and then go to **Table > Convert Cell to Graphic Cell**. This turns the cell into a graphic frame, and you can now go to **File > Place** and select your image to place it into the cell. You can still make manual adjustments to the cell after the image is placed. This is a really great way to give your tables some impact!

How Do I... Create a Header Row?

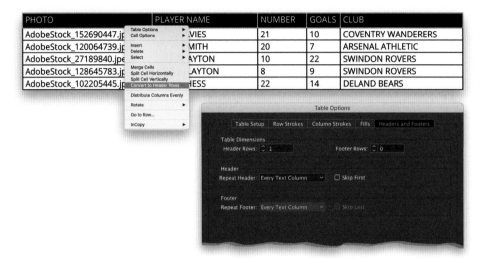

We often need our rows and columns to have headers that aren't part of the data and that will repeat if the table becomes long or difficult to follow. We can also create footers if necessary. To create a header row, highlight the row of cells you wish to be your header, and then Right-click in the cells and select **Convert to Header Rows** to make an instant change. Or you can choose **Table Options > Headers and Footers** from the same pop-up menu. This gives you more control over how many headers and footers you need and how often they are repeated. You can also convert a row of cells to a header row by selecting the cells and going to **Table > Convert Rows > To Header**.

?) How Do I... Move Columns and Rows Around?

PLAYER NAME	PHOTO	NUMBER	GOALS	CLUB	CARDS
BILLY DAVIES	AdobeStock_152690447.jpeg	21	10	COVENTRY WANDERERS	
SCOTT SMITH	AdobeStock_120064739.jpeg	20	7	ARSENAL ATHLETIC	
ELISE CLAYTON	AdobeStock_27189840.jpeg	10	22	SWINDON ROVERS	
FLEUR CLAYTON	AdobeStock_128645783.jpeg	8	9	SWINDON ROVERS	
AARON HESS	AdobeStock_102205445.jpeg	22	14	DELAND BEARS	

It's quite easy to move columns and rows around in a table without having to cut, copy, paste, or generally make a mess of your data. In this example we'll move a column, but you can use the same method to move a row up or down. Start by highlighting the column you want to move, and then hold the cursor over any part of the highlighted area. When the cursor changes to a black arrow with what looks like two tiny cells on top of each other, just click-and-drag the column into a new position. When it reaches the border of another column, you'll see a blue line appear, which means you can release the mouse and the column will be moved to that location within the table. Try it with a row too!

How Do I... Insert Rows and Columns?

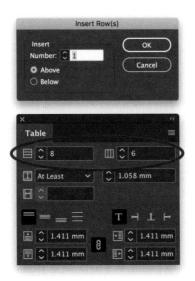

Before you insert a new row or column, you need to ensure that your table frame is large enough to accept the larger table; otherwise, you won't be able to see the full table and it will look like you haven't added anything. (When there is more content than will fit in the frame, you will see a small red square with a + in it down in the bottom-right corner of the frame.) Once you've enlarged your table frame, select the row or column next to where you want the new row or column to appear, and then Right-click and select **Insert > Row** or **Insert > Column**. You will see a dialog like the one shown above, which asks you how many rows or columns you want to insert and where you want to add them—above or below the selected row, or to the left or right of the selected column. You can also use the pop-up menus at the top of Table panel (circled above) to add or remove rows and columns, or you can go to **Table > Insert > Row** or **Table > Insert > Column**. Reverse the action by Right-clicking in a row or column and selecting **Delete > Row** or **Delete > Column**, or by selecting a row or column and going to **Table > Delete > Row** or **Table > Delete > Column**.

⑦ How Do I... Rotate Text in a Cell?

As usual, there are a couple of ways to do this. Start by selecting the cell or cells that contain the text you would like to rotate. Then go to **Table > Cell Options > Text** and in the dialog that opens, use the Text Rotation pop-up menu to select a degree of rotation. Alternatively, open the Table panel **(Window > Type & Tables > Table)** and look for the T icons in the lower-right area. Click on the T icon that is rotated to your liking, and the text in the selected cell will be rotated to the same degree.

How Do I... Align Text Vertically in a Cell?

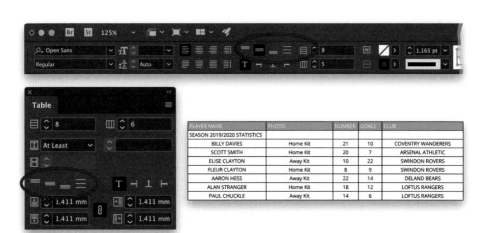

Once you've started placing text in a table (with no styles set), you will find that the text doesn't sit evenly in the cells. To get your text to sit smack dab in the vertical center of each cell, just select all your cells, and then click on the Align center icon (selected in the Control panel image at top) in the Control panel or Table panel. Or you may choose to align your text to the top or bottom of each cell.

? How Do I... Align Text Horizontally in a Cell?

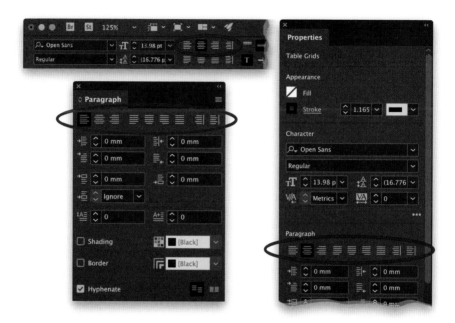

Once you've aligned your text vertically, you can also use the Paragraph alignment tool to align it to the left, center, or right of the cell, or to justify it so that it is aligned evenly on both sides. Select the cells that contain the text you wish to align, and then click on one of the Paragraph alignment icons in the Control panel, Paragraph panel, or Properties panel.

How Do I... Merge Cells?

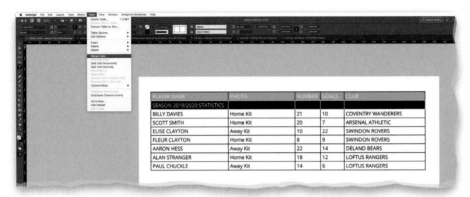

PLAYER NAME	PHOTO		NUMBER	GOALS	CLUB
SEASON 2019/2020 STATISTICS					
BILLY DAVIES	Home Kit		21	10	COVENTRY WANDERERS
SCOTT SMITH	Home Kit		20	7	ARSENAL ATHLETIC
ELISE CLAYTON	Away Kit		10	22	SWINDON ROVERS
FLEUR CLAYTON	Home Kit		8	9	SWINDON ROVERS
AARON HESS	Away Kit		22	14	DELAND BEARS
ALAN STRANGER	Home Kit		18	12	LOFTUS RANGERS
PAUL CHUCKLE	Away Kit		14	6	LOFTUS RANGERS

It's easy to merge cells in a table, both across rows and down columns. First, use the Type Tool **(T)** to select the cells you wish to merge. To select an entire row or column, hover your cursor over the left border of the row or the top border of the column, and when it turns into a thick black arrow, click once. You can also simply click-and-drag the cursor across the individual cells you wish to merge. Once the cells are selected, Right-click and select **Merge Cells** from the pop-up menu, or go to **Table > Merge Cells**. You can then set where you want your type to sit within the new single cell. In the example above, I merged the entire top row of cells. You can undo the merge by selecting the remaining individual cell and going to **Table > Unmerge Cells**.

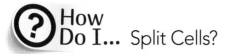

How Do I... Split Cells?

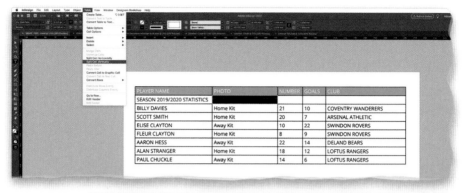

PLAYER NAME	PHOTO		NUMBER	GOALS	CLUB
SEASON 2019/2020 STATISTICS					
BILLY DAVIES	Home Kit		21	10	COVENTRY WANDERERS
SCOTT SMITH	Home Kit		20	7	ARSENAL ATHLETIC
ELISE CLAYTON	Away Kit		10	22	SWINDON ROVERS
FLEUR CLAYTON	Home Kit		8	9	SWINDON ROVERS
AARON HESS	Away Kit		22	14	DELAND BEARS
ALAN STRANGER	Home Kit		18	12	LOFTUS RANGERS
PAUL CHUCKLE	Away Kit		14	6	LOFTUS RANGERS

Splitting cells is kind of the opposite of merging cells. You can split a cell either vertically or horizontally. First, select the cell you wish to split, and then go to **Table > Split Cell Vertically** or **Split Cell Horizontally** (or Right-click on the selected cell and select one of these options). You can also find icons for these options in the Properties panel. You can do this with as many cells as you like. Merge cells and then split them. Split away!

How Do I... Fill Cells with Diagonal Lines?

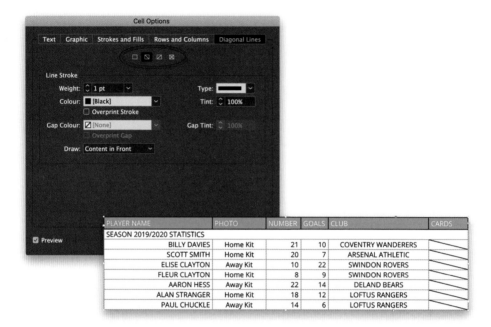

Let's say you have a cell with no data, but you don't want to leave it blank. Well, you don't have to. Instead, you can add a diagonal line or a cross through the cell. Select the cell(s) in which you want to add a line or cross, then Right-click and select **Cell Options > Diagonal Lines** (or go to **Table > Cell Options > Diagonal Lines**). In the Cell Options dialog, make sure the **Diagonal Lines** tab is selected, and then click on one of the icons at the top to select the style of line or cross you prefer. You can also adjust the line's weight, color, type, and more. Once you've adjusted it to your liking, click OK.

How Do I... Apply a Fill Color to a Cell?

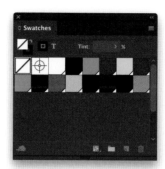

PLAYER NAME	PHOTO	NUMBER	GOALS	CLUB	CARDS
SEASON 2019/2020 STATISTICS					
BILLY DAVIES	Home Kit	21	10	COVENTRY WANDERERS	
SCOTT SMITH	Home Kit	20	7	ARSENAL ATHLETIC	
ELISE CLAYTON	Away Kit	10	22	SWINDON ROVERS	
FLEUR CLAYTON	Home Kit	8	9	SWINDON ROVERS	
AARON HESS	Away Kit	22	14	DELAND BEARS	
ALAN STRANGER	Home Kit	18	12	LOFTUS RANGERS	
PAUL CHUCKLE	Away Kit	14	6	LOFTUS RANGERS	

Let's fill some cells with color! As an example, we'll use a very basic method to manually create a single colored cell. Highlight the cell to which you want to add color, and go to any panel where a color swatch is found. (I like to use the Swatches panel, but you can also apply color to a cell from the Control panel, Properties panel, or Toolbar.) Make sure it's set to Fill (the little square icon), not Type (little T icon), select your color, and presto, you've colored a single cell. This is a really basic but quick way to apply color to a cell. Next we'll look at how to add a colored fill to multiple and alternate cells.

How Do I... Alternate Cell Fill Colors?

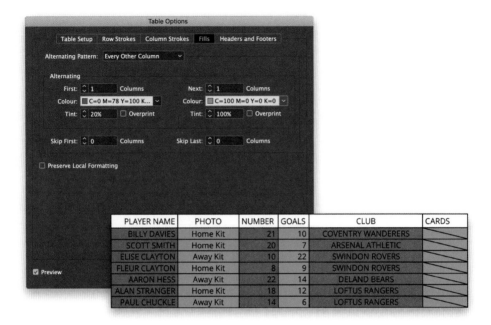

We've already covered how to add a single fill color to a single cell, but you can also create alternating fill colors. Select your table and go to **Table > Table Options > Alternating Fills**. In the dialog that opens, use the Alternating Pattern menu to choose how you want your fills to be applied. I chose **Every Other Column**. In the Alternating section of the dialog, select your first fill color (and tint if necessary), followed by your second color, and click OK. You now have a funky colored table with alternating fills.

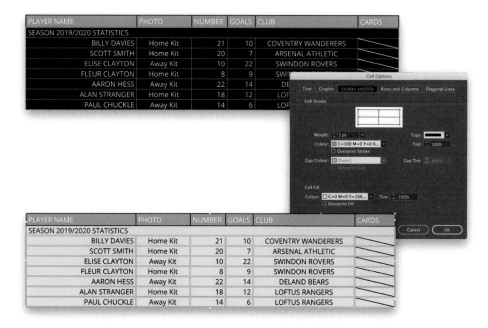

Let's look at how to quickly edit cell strokes and fills via a single dialog. Select the cells you wish to change and go to **Table > Cell Options > Strokes and Fills**. In the dialog that opens, you can make multiple changes to your table—and go crazy in the process, so beware—by adjusting stroke weight, stroke color, fill color, line type, and more. It's a powerful dialog! Just remember to think about all of these elements when you're creating a document with multiple tables, and make sure you get those style guides sorted!

How Do I... Add Table Borders?

Once you get your head around tables, you'll start to identify the various parts of a table. You now know about cells, strokes, fill colors, diagonal lines, and spacing, but here we'll be editing the actual table border itself—the very frame that houses the table. Start by selecting the entire table, and then go to **Table > Table Options > Table Setup**. We'll concentrate on the Table Border section of the dialog, where you can adjust the weight, color, line type, and tint of the border. You can see that I went a bit crazy in the example above—I told you that can happen if you aren't careful!— and gave the table a big, solid orange border just to highlight it. It will not win any awards—trust me!

How Do I... Create a Basic Table Style?

If you are going to be placing multiple tables with the same formatting in your document and you don't want to spend time formatting each one individually, just create a table style. This way you can select the style whenever you are creating a new table, and the correct formatting will automatically be applied. To create a new table style, go to **Window > Styles > Table Styles** to open the Table Styles panel. Then click on the panel menu and select **New Table Style**. In the New Table Style dialog, you can add any formatting options you need. Click on the tabs on the left side of the panel to access a variety of options, as follows: General (any cell styles you may already have); Table Setup (borders); Row Strokes (including any alternating row stroke patterns); Column Strokes (including any alternating column stroke patterns); and Fills (including any alternating fill requirements). Once you've adjusted the formatting to your liking, give your style a name and click OK. The style will now be available in the Table Styles panel. You can apply it to an existing table by selecting the table and clicking on the style name In the Table Styles panel. Or if you're creating a new table, you can select your style from the Table Style pop-up menu in the Create Table dialog (see page 198).

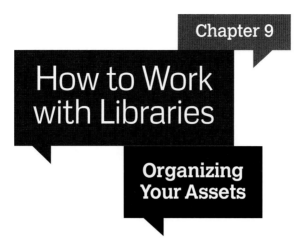

Chapter 9

How to Work with Libraries

Organizing Your Assets

The beauty of CC Libraries is that you can save images, color swatches, text styles, and other elements created in the various Creative Cloud desktop and mobile apps in a library, and then you can access these elements in InDesign, Photoshop, and Illustrator, as well as other Adobe apps, at any time. These assets can also be grouped to make searching for them much easier. You can even save content from a document to use in another one. In this chapter, we'll go through the various ways to add content to your a library, and how to manage your libraries and assets within them. When CC Libraries were first introduced, I couldn't use them quick enough! As someone who travels a lot and often receives requests to work on existing client files, having all my essential assets stored in CC Libraries means all I need is an internet connection, and I can access these files anywhere for any project. As a rule, I create libraries for all my client projects, and libraries for specific types of files, including assets downloaded from Adobe Stock. It is so easy to add, edit, and remove assets from CC Libraries that once you start using them, accessing them will become second nature. Another great benefit is being able to share libraries and have libraries shared with you, which is what the Adobe Creative Cloud is all about—creativity and collaboration. By the end of this chapter, I hope you start building your own CC Library workflow and that you use it like a champ!

InDesign Fun Fact #10
Although InDesign is at version CC 2019 (at the time of writing), it is actually version 14.0. Since the first version, it has gone through 27 versions (including updates like 11.1, 11.2, 11.3, 11.4) to get where it is today. It's also had some fun code names—look for those in the chapter 12 introduction.

How Do I... Create a CC Library?

Libraries are one of my favorite features in Adobe CC applications. The beauty of libraries is that you can save images, color swatches, text styles, and other elements created in the various Creative Cloud desktop and mobile apps in a library, and then you can access these elements across all of the apps at any time. Go to **Window > CC Libraries** to open the panel. If this is the first time you are using Libraries, then you won't have any assets or folders set up, so the first thing you need to do is create a new library. To do this, open the pop-up menu near the top of the panel (below the Search field) and select **+ Create New Library** at the bottom of the menu. You can see in the example image above that I already have multiple libraries, but I can always add more. Type a name for your library into the Create New Library field, and then click on Create. You'll notice that your new library is now selected in the pop-up menu near the top of the panel, and you can start adding assets to it. You can make multiple libraries for different projects.

How Do I... Access My Other Libraries?

This tip is pretty simple, but it's also a good guide for naming strategies. You can access all of your libraries from within the CC Libraries panel via the pop-up menu near the top, just below the Search field. You want to name your libraries efficiently so that you can identify them quickly. They will be listed alphabetically, but try to avoid leaving them named "My Library" because you will end up with multiple folders with the same name, which isn't helpful to anyone! It also isn't specific, so it'll be hard to remember what's in it when you're looking at a long list of libraries. I prefix my client libraries CLIENT_<CLIENT NAME or PROJECT> so that all my client folders appear together. There are lots of great naming strategies, but that's one I use often.

(?) How Do I... Add an Image to My Library?

Adding images from an external source to a library is relatively easy. With the CC Libraries panel open and the required library selected, just select some images from a folder on your computer and drag them directly onto the panel. If you are adding multiple images, you'll see a little red icon showing the number of images you are adding. After a couple of seconds, they'll appear in your panel, available at full resolution and ready to use in your documents. You can continue to add more images—including PSD, JPG, PNG, AI, EPS, and TIFF files—at any time.

? How Do I... Add an Image from My Document to a Library?

It's really simple to add an image you have already placed into your document to your library. Make sure the library to which you want to add the image is selected in the CC Libraries panel, and then simply drag the image off your page onto the panel. A plus sign will appear in the panel, indicating that you are adding an element. Alternatively, you can click on the image in your document to select it, and then click on the small + sign in the bottom-left corner of the CC Libraries panel. Click on the pop-up Graphic button, and your image is added to the library. Now, there are a couple of things to consider when using these methods. You'll be saving the image exactly as it appears in your document, along with any amendments you've made to it. For example, if you resize the frame and add a stroke, that's what gets saved when you drag the frame into the CC Libraries panel. If you want to add just the image, untouched, click in the middle "donut" ring of the image (with the default settings, the frame of the whole image will be brown), and you can now drag the image into the CC Libraries panel, or use the + Graphic option, to add the image to your library without any amendments.

How Do I... Add Type Styles to My Library?

You can add paragraph or character styles to your CC Libraries and share these across documents and devices, or with other users. Your options are to add styles from the text in your document (above left), from the Paragraph Styles or Character Styles panels (above center), or from the New Character Style or New Paragraph Style dialogs (above right). Before you add anything, make sure the library to which you want to add the styles is selected in the CC Libraries panel. To add a style from your document text, just select the text frame where the style is applied, and then click on the + icon in the bottom-left corner of the CC Libraries panel and select **Paragraph Style** or **Character Style** from the menu that opens. To add a style from one of the styles panels, open the required panel **(Window > Styles > Character Styles or Paragraph Styles)** and select the style(s) you want to add (you can select more than one style at a time). Then click on the small cloud icon in the bottom-left corner of that panel to Add selected style to my current library. You may want to add a style to your library right when you create it. To do so, open the panel menu in the Character Styles or Paragraph Styles panel and select **New Character/Paragraph Style**. In the dialog that opens, choose your style settings and add a check mark next to Add to CC Library near the bottom-left corner of the dialog. You can add the style to any library by choosing it from the pop-up menu next to Add to CC Library. Very flexible, indeed!

How Do I... Add Typed Content to CC Libraries?

If you have some typed content that you plan to use over and over again in other projects—such as contact info or social media links, for example—you can type out your text, style it accordingly, and drag the entire text frame onto your CC Libraries panel. Or you can select the text frame in your document, click on the **+** sign in the bottom-left corner of the CC Libraries panel, select **Text** from the menu, and click Add. The typed content is now available for use across all Adobe CC applications.

How Do I... Edit Typed Content Once Its in a Library?

Double-click on the type asset in your CC Libraries panel and it will open in a new InDesign window. Make your changes, and then close that file. This automatically updates the type and you'll see the change in the asset thumbnail. If you want to make a separate instance of the type so that you have two versions, Right-click on the type asset and select **Duplicate**, before you make any changes to the original type asset. Then edit the duplicate version.

How Do I... Apply an Asset from My Library to My Document?

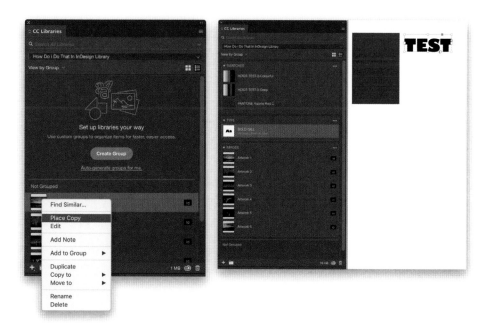

Once you've added assets to your CC Libraries folder, you can quickly apply them to your document. For images, it's as simple as Right-clicking on the image and selecting **Place Copy**. If a frame is selected in your document, the image will automatically be placed into that frame; if not, your place cursor will be loaded and you can drag out the image in any location and at whatever size you choose. You can also place an image by clicking-and-dragging the image onto your document. To apply any other assets, such as color swatches or character styles, just select the item to which you want to apply them, and then click on the asset in the panel. Using CC Libraries can save you so much time—that's why I love them!

How Do I... Delete Items from a Library?

This is really, really simple and doesn't require much explanation. Just select the asset(s) you want delete in the CC Libraries panel, Right-click, and select **Delete**. Or select the asset(s) and click on the tiny trash can icon in the bottom-right corner of the panel.

?) How Do I... View Items I Previously Deleted from My Libraries?

Open the CC Libraries panel menu and select **View Deleted Items**. This takes you to your Libraries web page in a browser, where you will see previously deleted items from your library. From here, you can restore or permanently delete an asset by clicking on the checkbox in its top-left corner, and then clicking on Restore or Permanently Delete near the top-right corner of the web page. Once an item is restored, it will appear back in the Library from which it was deleted.

How
Do I... Create Groups to Organize My Library?

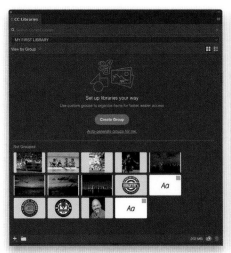

Near the top of your CC Libraries panel, just below the library name pop-up menu, you'll see either View by Type or View by Group with a downward-pointing arrow next to it. If this is set to View by Type, click on the arrow and select **View by Group**. If you have not yet created any groups, you should see an area in the top half of the CC Libraries panel prompting you to create groups to organize the items in your library. You can click on Create Group to set up a custom group and add what you like to it, or you can click on Auto-generate groups for me (just below the Create Group button), and InDesign will automatically create groups for type, images, vectors, swatches, etc. These automatically generated groups will also be visible when View by Type is selected. You can also create a group by clicking on the Create Group icon (looks like a file folder) in the bottom-left corner of the panel. Then just drag any existing assets into the new group. Any asset can be added, regardless of whether or not it's already in an existing group. As a huge fan of libraries, I would highly recommend you use this feature to keep your assets organized. This is especially helpful when you're using CC Libraries in other applications.

How Do I... Move, Copy, Rename, or Delete Groups in My Library?

Once you've created a group of assets, just look for the three dots in the top-right corner of the group. Click on that and you'll be presented with the following options:

Copy to—Select another library into which you want to copy the group.

Move to—Select another library into which you want to move the group.

Rename Group—Give your group a new name.

Delete Group—This releases the assets from the group and leaves them in the library.

Delete Group and Contents—This deletes both the group and the assets within it.

How Do I... Use CC Libraries to Build Brand Folders?

This tip is really just a suggestion for one helpful way to use CC Libraries. Creating folders or libraries is a great way to organize brand assets. I create a library for each project I work on, and in it are all the assets I need for that client, including swatches, styles, images, text, and more. And of course, once I create a library, I use the group function to separate all the assets. This has really helped when I am on the road and a client needs something I'm working on. I can quickly access all the elements and use them or share them. Yep, we can share our libraries; that's covered in this chapter too!

How Do I... Search in CC Libraries?

InDesign makes it easy to search for an asset in your libraries or search for a resource on Adobe Stock (see the next tip for info about Adobe Stock). Click on the downward-pointing arrow at the far-right end of the Search field at the top of the CC Libraries panel, and select from **Adobe Stock, Current Library**, or **All Libraries**. Now you can type whatever you're looking for into the Search field and your results will be displayed below. In the example above, I searched for "red" and got a color swatch as well as some graphics that have red in them. Now, let's say you search all libraries to find a particular asset, and you want to move that asset into your current library. Guess what? You can! Right-click on the file and select **Copy to** or **Move to**, and then select the library where you want that asset to appear. I told you libraries were brilliant! And if I didn't, well, they are brilliant!

How Do I... Use Adobe Stock Assets in CC Libraries?

Another great benefit of the Creative Cloud (and there are many) is the addition of Adobe Stock and its easy integration into the apps. Straight from the CC Libraries panel you can find Adobe Stock assets to use in your projects and save in your library. Go to the Search bar at the top of the CC Libraries panel, click on the downward-pointing arrow at the far-right end, and select **Adobe Stock**. Type in what you are looking for, and browse the results in your CC Libraries panel. To save a preview of an image to test in your project, hover over it with your cursor and click on the cloud icon that appears. The preview will be added to your current library. Or you can license the stock resource and have it saved straight to your current library by clicking on the shopping cart icon. If an image is an Adobe Stock Premium image it will state that on the thumbnail. This is another great way to gather some potential assets to use at a later time. You can search on the go and test your previews when you have time to work on your project, and then you can Right-click on the resource and license it straight from the library.

How Do I... Share My Libraries with Others?

 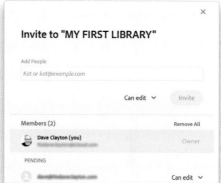

Once you have created a library, you can share it with other CC users. Depending on the type of access you give them, they will be able to view, use, edit, and/or rename the library. If a folder is shared with you, then you can also pass it on and share it with another user. Be careful what you share and receive, and always check the licensing on files. To share a library in your CC Libraries panel, select a library from the pop-up menu near the top (below the Search field), and then open the panel menu and choose **Collaborate**. An internet browser will open up to an Adobe page where you can provide an email address and message for the person with whom you want to share the library. Choose **Can edit** or **Can view** from the pop-up menu at the bottom of the dialog, and then click Invite. The person will receive an invite to the library via email (see the next tip to find out how to accept a shared library). Until that person accepts the invitation, they'll be listed under "Pending" in your invite dialog.

How Do I... Accept a Shared Library?

If someone has shared a library with you, you'll receive an email stating whom the invite is from and the name of the shared library. Make sure you are logged into your Creative Cloud account to access the file. When you click on Accept the Invitation, you'll be taken to a web page to log in to your Creative Cloud account, if you aren't already logged in. There you will see your library files and an Updates and Requests notification with the details of the shared file. (*Note:* Notifications are indicated by a small red dot with the number of notifications on the bell icon near the top-right corner of the web page; click on the bell to open them.) Now all you have to do is click on Accept to get access to the folder. This new library will now automatically show up in your list of available libraries.

?How Do I... Leave a Shared Library?

If you receive an invite to a library, but for some reason you don't need access to it, or if you accept an invite but no longer want access to it, then you can decline the invite or leave the shared library. To decline, just hit Decline instead of Accept on the Updates and Requests notification, and that's the end of that. To leave a shared library that you've already accepted, open the library pop-up menu at the top of the CC Libraries panel and select the library you want to leave. Then open the panel menu and choose **Leave "[library name]."** (*Note:* If you have Edit rights for the library, you can also choose to rename the library from this menu, but if Rename is grayed out, as in the example above, it means you only have View access.) You can also leave a shared library from the Adobe Creative Cloud web page. Once you're logged in, click on Shared with You, put a check mark in the box for the library you want to leave, and click on Leave in the upper-right corner of the web page.

Note: You can't delete a library folder that you don't own (one that's been shared with you); you can only leave it. If you created the library and shared it with someone else, then you can delete it.

How Do I... Delete a Library?

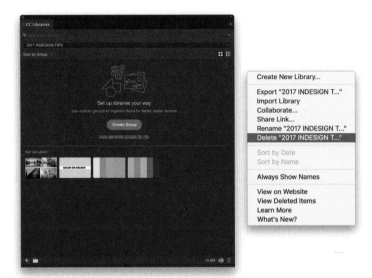

To delete a library, just select it from the pop-up menu near the top of the CC Libraries panel, open the panel menu, and select **Delete "[library name]."** Like all good software, InDesign will ask you if you are sure. Select Delete, or Cancel if you change your mind. This will remove that library and all its assets, so make sure you've moved any assets you need to another library folder.

How Do I... Find the File Size of Items in My Library?

If you start adding assets to your library and need to know how large your library is, just look at the bottom strip of the panel and you'll see the total library file size. If you select an individual item, you'll see the file size for that item, and if you select multiple items, you'll see the collective size. You can also hover your cursor over an image, and you'll see a pop-up information window with all the info about that file, including dimensions and file size.

Chapter 10

How to Save and Output Files

Printing and Exporting Your Documents

We're getting to the business end of this book now. We've learned all these great skills to help us become InDesign pros, but what do we do with all this amazing work we've created? We need to output it for others to see. As I've said all along, InDesign is the tool for creating documents, and in a world where I still love print and books still rule (!), we have InDesign to make this part of the process the best in the business. I've also made it clear that InDesign isn't just for print; we can still output great documents with interactivity for the web. Let's start with print. I'll walk you through how to save your documents and what formats are available to you. We'll look at how to set up bleeds and print marks; how to create professional looking PDFs; how to print selected pages from a document; how to save templates for future use; how to package up your files to share with others, or back them up for future use; and more. Saving, export, and output is an important part of sharing and publishing your work, but more importantly, it's about controlling how your work is saved and stored. As you become more proficient in InDesign and start creating bigger and more complicated files, it will be so important to have a save, store, and export regime to manage your important documents. As an additional tip, I would highly recommend you learn more about the world of PDF—it's an essential and incredibly powerful tool.

InDesign Fun Fact #11

More than 91 million unique PDF files are generated in InDesign every year.

How Do I... Save My Document as an INDD File?

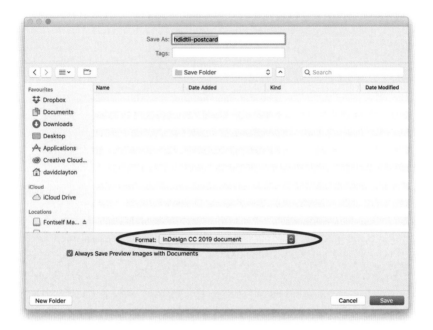

So, what's an INDD file? This is the default file type for the current version of InDesign. To save your document as an INDD file, go to **File > Save/Save As/Save a Copy** to bring up the Save dialog. Here, you get to name your file and decide where you want to save it, and there several file format options in the Format (PC: Save as Type) pop-up menu near the bottom of the dialog: **InDesign CC 2019 document / InDesign CC 2019 / InDesign CS4 or later (IDML)**. Select the first option, and your document will be saved as a native INDD file. This means it will only open with the current version of InDesign. To save a file that can be opened in a version of InDesign that is older than the one you are currently using, well, check out the next tip!

How Do I... Save a Document to be Opened in an Older Version of InDesign?

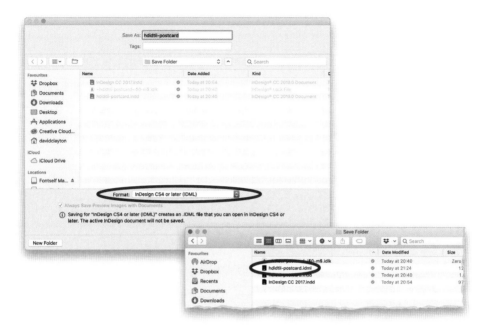

One of the quirks of InDesign is that an INDD file saved in the current version of the software can't be opened in older versions. In order to save a document created in the current version of InDesign so that it can be opened by an older version of the software, the document has to be saved as an IDML file. If you want the technical reason for this, here it is: IDML stands for Adobe InDesign Markup Language. IDML is an XML representation of an InDesign document or its components. This is the interchange format for Adobe InDesign. Knowing this technical information isn't going to make you any wiser, but it will make you understand that for anyone you may be working with who doesn't have the same version of InDesign as you (i.e., any older version), you should always save an IDML file. Just go to **File > Save As** and select **InDesign CS4 or later (IDML)** from the Format (PC: Save as Type) pop-up menu near the bottom of the dialog. This tip will save you from having to go back and resave a document later. But Dave, what if I saved an INDD file in, say, InDesign CC 2017, and I want to open it in CC 2019? Can I do that? Yes, yes you can. The latest version of the software can open an INDD file created and saved in an older Creative Cloud version—just not the other way around.

How Do I... Save a Copy of My Document?

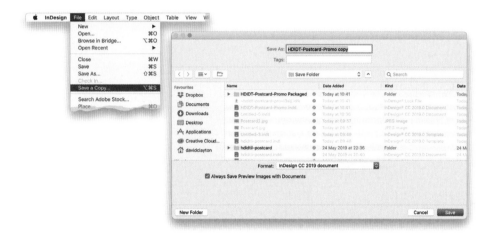

Let's say you are working on a document and you need to send the current version to a colleague, but you don't want to actually save the current file and start renaming it. The best way to do this is to go to **File > Save a Copy**. This enables you to save a copy of the current version of the document with a filename that you may use for tracking versions sent to other collaborators, and you can maintain your own copy with its original filename. It is a file-saving option most people look past, but it's actually a time saver because you don't have to "Save As," rename the file, close it, and then reopen the one you were originally working on.

How Do I... Save a Document as a Template?

You can make your own templates or download them from Adobe Stock. Your template might include items such as ruler guides, page numbers, mastheads, text panels, and styles you want to use for each issue of a newsletter, for example. If you create a document and wish to save it as a template, there's a quick shortcut: when saving, just add the letter "t" to the end of the file extension (i.e., .indd becomes .inddt). Alternatively, you can go to **File > Save As** and select **InDesign CC 2019 Template** from the Format (PC: Save as Type) pop-up menu. This means the file is saved as a template, and the next time you open that file it will force you to save it as something else so that you don't accidentally write over a file you wish to use again and again. To open a template you have downloaded or saved, go to **File > New > Document** and click on Saved at the top of the New Document dialog, and any templates you have saved will be shown. You can also go to **File > Open** and browse for saved templates on your computer.

? How Do I... Print Individual Pages or Spreads?

Have you ever been working on a multipage document and wanted to print a page or two instead of the entire document? In the Print dialog you are able to dictate which pages you wish to print; however, it's a bit tricky if you don't know how to select the page ranges for multiple-page documents. But don't worry, there's a cool little trick to make it an easier process using the Pages panel. Just open up the Pages panel **(Window > Pages)** and click on the first page you want to print to select it. **Command-click (PC: Ctrl-click)** on any other pages you wish to print (if you're not printing the whole document). Once you've selected your pages, Right-click on any selected page and choose **Print Pages.** This brings up the Print dialog, and you'll see the pages you selected have automatically been listed in Range field. From there you can make any other changes to your print job, such as number of copies, marks and bleeds, and print size.

How Do I... Save a Document as a Standard Print-Only PDF?

First, a quick caveat: the world of PDFs and prepress printing is huge and goes beyond the scope of this book. Here, I am going to show you how to save a file as a PDF with default settings. If you want to further pursue the world of PDFs, I suggest you find a good local printer and a comprehensive book on printing. Okay, let's export our file to PDF. There are a couple of ways to do this, but we'll use the default method. There are two options for this in the File menu: **Export** and **Adobe PDF Presets**. We'll stick with the basic one—Export—to show you how to get to the PDF stage. Once you select Export, you'll get a Save As dialog where you can name the file and choose where you want to export to (i.e., where to save the file). In the Format (PC: Save as Type) menu, select **PDF Print**, then click Save. This opens up the Export Adobe PDF dialog. This might scare you, but don't panic! First, I always open the Adobe PDF Preset menu and choose **High Quality Print**. I want a high-quality PDF, and it's much easier to send bigger files these days. Next, I go to the Standard menu and choose **PDF/X-1a:2001** because it's the best start to ensure the PDF has all the elements it needs. (*Note:* For PDF/X-1a, all fonts need to be embedded and all images need to be CMYK or spot colors.) The only other thing I do is put a check mark in the box next to View PDF after Exporting. We are going to cover a couple of other elements in this chapter, but we'll leave them for now. Click Export and your document will be exported to PDF and saved in the location you chose, and a preview will open up in Acrobat.

You know all that stuff we just did in the previous tip? That's for a print document. You can also create PDFs for digital output so they can be viewed and read online and include clickable links. This time you need to go to **File > Export**, and in the Save As dialog, open the Format (PC: Save as Type) menu and choose **Adobe PDF (Interactive)**. This will give you the Export to Interactive PDF dialog, which has a much simpler layout than the one in the previous tip. Here you can decide how many pages of your document you wish to export (if it's a multi-page document), and whether you want it to export as individual pages or as spreads, like in a magazine with facing pages. You also have some Viewing options. Once you become a bit of an expert, you'll use more of these settings, but for now we'll stick to **Default** for both the View and Layout settings. There are also Page Transition options—we'll leave this menu as is for now, but I suggest experimenting with these options later to find one that suits your needs. Click Export, and you've saved an interactive PDF. Here's something to think about: it's only really interactive if you give it some interactive elements, such as hyperlinked URLs or a call to action, such as "Click to email."

How Do I... Automatically Retain the Document Filename When Exporting to PDF?

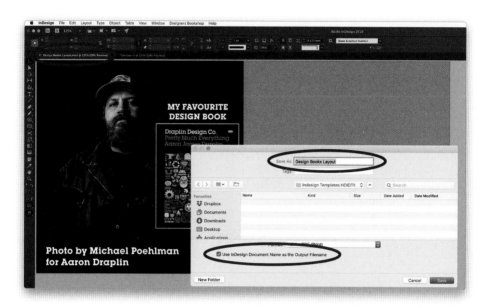

When you are exporting a document, you can retain the filename of the InDesign document you are working in. Go to **File > Export**, and in the Save As dialog, put a check mark next to Use InDesign Document Name as the Output Filename (near the bottom of the dialog). Even with this option checked, you can rename the document something different, but the next time you export, the default name will be the document name. Continue on with the exporting directions from the previous two tips, "How Do I Save to Standard Print-Only PDF?" and "How Do I Save to Digital-Format PDF?"

How Do I... Export Individual PDF Pages?

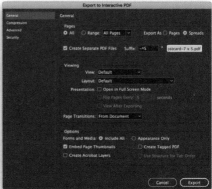

With the release of InDesign CC 2018 and subsequent versions came the ability to export an InDesign document to PDF and create separate PDFs for each page or spread. We no longer need to open the saved PDF in Adobe Acrobat and split it up into multiple files manually. That was a royal pain in the backside. Worry no more, now there's a checkbox for this very task, and it's about time too! To create separate PDF files, choose **File > Export** and in the Save As dialog, open the Format (PC: Save as Type) menu and choose either the **Adobe PDF (Print)** or **Adobe PDF (Interactive)** format; it works with both. In the Export Adobe PDF dialog, put a check mark next to Create Separate PDF Files. It's ideal to use the Suffix field to define what information gets added to the end of the exported PDF filename so you can identify which pages are which. Click on the little arrow to the right of the Suffix field and choose whether you want to use **Incremental Numbers, Page Number,** or **Page Size.** The filename field to the right of the Suffix field automatically takes the InDesign filename of the original document, but this can be edited if necessary.

How Do I... Protect a PDF with a Password?

There may be times when you want to send a PDF to someone, but you don't want just anyone to be able to open or edit the document. To ensure that only the intended recipients are able to open or edit your PDF, you can assign a password to your exported document. When using the **File > Export** option (see pages 249 and 250 for more on exporting to PDF), make sure you click on the Security tab in the Export Adobe PDF dialog. Place a check mark next to Require a password to open the document, and enter a password in the field below (make sure you remember it!). This prevents anyone other than a password holder from opening the document. In the Permissions field of that same dialog, you can also add a password to restrict printing, editing, and other tasks. Again, check the box for that option, and then decide on the level of control a password holder can have in terms of editing and/or printing. When you are happy with the security of your document, click Export.

How Do I... Show Marks and Bleeds for Printing?

If you need to print out a document or you want the recipient to see the trim and bleed marks, then you can add this to your exported PDF. In the Export Adobe PDF dialog **(File > Export)**, click on the Marks and Bleeds tab. Here you can decide which marks are visible in your document by simply checking the boxes for each one. You can also tell the PDF to use the document Bleed and Slug settings. (*Note:* See page 42 for information on how to set up bleed marks for your document.) Click Export to export your document to a PDF with the selected marks and bleeds. You can see the trim marks in the corners of the example above.

How Do I... Create a PDF Preset?

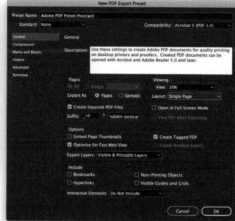

There may be times when you have a bunch of settings you wish to apply to a PDF export, and then want to use them over and over again. Here's how to create a preset so you can do that easily. With your document open, go to **File > Adobe PDF Presets > Define**. This opens up the Adobe PDF Presets dialog, where you'll see a list of existing presets at the top. We'll click New. In the New PDF Export Preset dialog, choose any settings you wish to include in your PDF preset, give it a name, and click OK. This saves your preset, and the next time you go to **File > Adobe PDF Presets**, you'll see the one you created in the list of available presets (below Define). If you wish to edit an existing preset, simply open the Adobe PDF Presets dialog **(File > Adobe PDF Presets > Define)**, select the preset you want to modify, and click Edit. Make your changes, and then click Save. To apply a preset, just go to **File > Export** as you normally would, choose **Adobe PDF (Print)** from the Format (PC: Save as Type) menu, and click Save. In the Export to PDF dialog, click on the Adobe PDF Preset pop-up menu at the very top, select your new preset, and click Export. It's as simple as that!

How Do I... Export to Image Formats (Like JPG or PNG)?

Occasionally you may need to export your document, or pages from the document, as something other than a PDF, such as an image file. You have multiple options available within the Export command. Go to **File > Export**, name your document, and from the Format (PC: Save as Type) menu, you can select **JPEG** or **PNG** to save your document as an image. If you select JPEG, you will be presented with an Export JPEG dialog, which allows you to choose which pages you wish to export; the quality and resolution of the files; the color space used; and whether to include bleed settings. This is a really useful way to create small-file-size versions of your document to email to others, or even to design something in InDesign specifically for export to an image format that can be posted on the web or social media.

How Do I... Package My Files?

Packaging your InDesign file rounds up all of the various elements (including images, vector logos, any other graphic format files, and fonts) and saves everything in a folder. It's basically like making copies to send with the file, but it also creates a link integrity that will work when the file is opened elsewhere. To start the process, go to **File > Package**. In the Package dialog, you'll see some information about your file, as well as tabs down the left side of the dialog for other elements of the document, such as Font info, Links info, Colors and Inks, Print Settings, etc. Before you package your file, ensure you have the "No Errors" green light at the bottom of the InDesign Workspace! Click Package, and in the next dialog you'll be asked to name the packaged folder and choose where you wish to save it. You'll also need to select which elements of the document you wish to include. I always leave everything checked, except for Use Document Hyphenation Exceptions Only. I usually recommend setting Select PDF Preset to **High Quality Print**, but you can also select a preset you've made for that document. Now click Package. You will see a warning that advises you about font software licensing. Click OK, but remember, the fonts in the document are licensed to you only; they are not for others to take and use for themselves! Now go to the folder where you saved your package and check to make sure all the items are in there. You'll have a PDF, the INDD file, and the fonts and images in their own folders. DO NOT MOVE ANYTHING, OR YOU WILL BREAK THE LINKS.

How Do I... Share Adobe Fonts with a Packaged File?

That's sort of a trick question because the answer is, you can't. The packaging process will round up any fonts on your system that are used in the document, but if you used any Adobe Fonts, the recipient of the package will receive a notification and they will have to download or license the font(s) themselves. This notification is especially useful when you're collaborating with a studio or print shop that is also on Creative Cloud because they can automatically download those fonts as part of their subscription. You can see which Adobe Fonts are used in the document by clicking on the Fonts tab on the left side of the Package dialog. In your list of included fonts, the Adobe Fonts will show as Status: Activated, Protected: Yes.

How Do I... Publish My Document Online?

You can publish any InDesign document online and share it with your social networks, via email, or even as a standalone web page. You can also embed the document into any web page or blog. The HTML version of your document is viewable on all desktops, tablets, and smartphones, and it will support all the interactivity you may have included in the InDesign document. First, ensure your document is complete and error-free, and then click the **Publish Online** button near the top-right corner of the application frame (or go to **File > Publish Online**). In the dialog that appears, click the **General** tab and give your document a name and a brief description. Select the page range—specific pages or the whole document—and decide if the viewer will see single pages or spreads. Finally, you can check an option that allows the viewer to download the document as a PDF, and whether the share and embed options will be available to the viewer for sharing elsewhere. Now click the **Advanced** tab and select the image you wish to use for the preview or cover image. Choose the Image quality settings for all of the images in the document, and the quality of the available PDF download. Click OK to begin publishing. Once your file has been uploaded, click **View Document** to view it in a browser. You can also click **Copy** to copy a link to the file so you can share it with others, and you can share the online document on social media channels such as Facebook or Twitter, or via email, by clicking on the buttons included. (*Note:* You may have to log into your social media channels to enable the sharing options.)

Chapter 11

Plug-ins, Scripts, and Other Cool Stuff

Adding More to Your Toolbox

InDesign is an incredible application and part of an ever-growing creative community. It is THE professional, industry tool and the benchmark for publishing. Yes, there are alternatives available, but they're all striving to be as good as InDesign has been for 20 years. And there are creatives out there making additional tools for InDesign, such as scripts and plug-ins (many free and some you'll need to pay for), that enable us to perform functions quicker and easier, which gives us more precious time to create and earn a living. In this chapter we'll talk about where to find these scripts and plug-ins and how to install them. We'll go hunting for some fun Easter eggs in InDesign, some of which are incredibly useful! We'll look at some professional additions to InDesign, such as the powerful Extensis products made especially for the creative and publishing sector. These are tools that have been at the leading edge in the publishing market since 1993. We'll take a quick look at Grid Calculator Pro, a great tool for setting up professional grid systems for your files, and we'll check out Fontself (one of my personal favorites), which is a brilliant tool for making your own typefaces and fonts to use in your InDesign documents. I'll also show you how to make QR codes right in InDesign. Then we'll look at where else you can find resources for both InDesign and general design needs. There are some excellent training resources out there, including my own InDesign classes on KelbyOne.com, and more content over at InDesign Secrets, a site run by David Blatner and Anne Marie Concepcion. There are lots of creative people out there creating and sharing content to make the world of InDesign and publishing a better place. I hope you've found that this book has become a part of that!

InDesign Fun Fact #12

Before changing to simple version numbers, some of InDesign's codenames have included Shuksan, K2, Sherpa, Annapunna, DragonTail, FireDrake, Cobalt, Basil, Rocket, Athos, Citius, and Sirius.

How Do I... Find Great Plug-ins for InDesign?

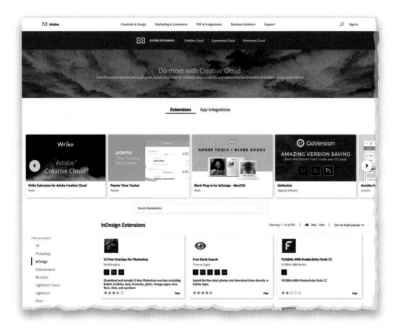

Plug-ins are additional software programs developed by Adobe as well as third-party software developers. They add additional features to InDesign and have to comply with Adobe standards. They can range from general automation processes to productivity tools, font management tools, or all sorts of special effects. Most of the features you use in InDesign are provided by plug-ins. Once you've installed a plug-in, it will usually appear as additional options in the menus, dialogs, or panels in your workspace. In this chapter, we will look at a couple of my favorites. There is additional information on plug-ins on the Adobe website, and a good place to find them is the Adobe Exchange website. Each plug-in can have its own method of installation, so check the instructions for each one you decide to install.

Find a list of third-party developers and their plug-ins at:
https://helpx.adobe.com/indesign/plug-ins.html

You can find more great plug-ins here:
https://www.adobeexchange.com/creativecloud.indesign.html#product

How Do I... Install Scripts?

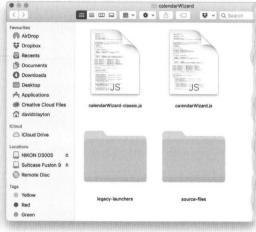

Scripts perform automated functions to help you achieve a specific task in your document, such as repair or format text, and provide tools that aren't natively found in InDesign or that give you more control than what currently exists in InDesign. Some basic scripts are included in the Scripts panel **(Window > Utilities > Scripts)**, but you can find many others by searching online. Once you're familiar with the structure of scripts, you can begin to code your own, but for now, we'll focus on ones that already exist. First, download the script onto your computer (please ensure you have antivirus security on your system, as I cannot vouch for each and every link you find, but I do recommend trusted sites like InDesignSecrets), and if it's delivered as a zip file, unzip it. You should now have a folder with a plain text file (and possibly other files that make up the script) whose filename extension could be any of the following:

- Javascript files have a .js, .jsx, .jsxbin extension
- Applescript files are Mac-only and have an .applescript or .scpt extension
- Visual Basic files are Windows-only and have a .vbs extension

Now just follow the installation instructions and enjoy the new functionality they bring! Some useful websites for finding scripts:

http://www.gilbertconsulting.com/resources-scripts.html

https://indesignsecrets.com/resources/plug-ins-and-scripts

How Do I... Run a Script?

There are a couple of ways to install scripts in InDesign: via the application folder or the user script folder. The second method is the quickest: just open the Scripts panel **(Window > Utilities > Scripts)**, Right-click on User (that's the best option for scripts that you've downloaded), and choose **Reveal in Finder (PC: Reveal in Windows Explorer)**. This opens up a folder called Scripts Panel. Move the scripts you've downloaded into this folder by dragging them over from the Downloads folder. Any script you place into the Scripts Panel folder will show up straight away in InDesign, under User in the Scripts panel; there's no need to restart the app. In the image above, you can see that I've installed my calendar script (calendarWizard.js) from the previous tip. Now that it is installed, all you have to do to run the new script is open a document in InDesign, open up the Scripts panel, and double-click on the script name. Keep in mind that some scripts require you to select an object in the document before you can run them because they affect the selected item. Once you get the hang of using scripts you'll be adding them to your creative arsenal in no time—work smarter, not harder!

How Do I... Use Extensis Tools for Font Management?

Extensis is an industry leading company that has been around for many years, providing professional font management (and digital asset) plug-ins. These plug-ins offer a more sophisticated method of organizing and managing the hundreds or even thousands of fonts on your system or your network, which is particularly handy if you are part of a design studio with multiple font users, for instance. They also have powerful font search functionality, and when you have a lot of fonts, this kind of tool can save hours of time and also protect you from using unlicensed fonts. Recently Extensis added a font search feature that I think is not only pretty amazing, but really useful too (see next tip). If you are anything like me, you are a digital hoarder and have hundreds of fonts. Being able to tag fonts by client name is incredibly helpful because you can then search a font and see if it is attributed to a client, or search a client and see which fonts are attributed to them—a powerful timesaver!

Check out Suitcase Fusion, a great font management system (https://www.extensis .com/suitcase-fusion-free-trial/). Just follow the instructions on the Extensis website. They offer a free trial, but the overall commercial license is around $120, which is affordable for professional font management.

Note: I'm not affiliated with Extensis. I'm just a happy customer!

How Do I... Use Extensis Tools to Find Fonts in Documents?

Extensis includes a feature in their Suitcase Fusion app called Document Tracking, whereby you can search your computer for InDesign files that use a specific font. With Suitcase Fusion running, you can add multiple InDesign (and Photoshop and Illustrator) documents to it and instruct the software to use document tracking. Then when you click on a file, the software will display what fonts that document is using. If a font is no longer on your system, the software will flag it with a warning. There's much more power to this tool, but I love this feature! If you're creating professional documents for clients, it's worth building the price of this app license into your rates to help with this requirement. I keep all the documents I have ever made in InDesign, just in case a client ever comes back and asks me to make changes to an old document. Sometimes that means a change to the style guide, and if it's a font replacement, you never know which of those old documents uses old fonts. Here is a useful video explaining how to use this feature: https://vimeo.com/295199547.

How Do I... Generate a QR Code?

It's a lot simpler for people to read QR codes these days, as more smartphones have a QR reader built into their internal camera. Let's look at how to set up and edit a QR code. With a document open, go to **Object > Generate QR Code**. In the dialog that opens, click on the Content tab and select the Type of link you are generating from the pop-up menu at the top. Your choices are Web Hyperlink, Plain Text, Text Message, Email, or Business Card. We won't go through all the options here, but we'll look at the main one, Web Hyperlink, and then you can play around with the others and test them out. Select **Web Hyperlink** from the Type menu, type the full URL for the webpage you would like to link to in the field below (in this example, https://heshootshedraws.com), and click OK. Next, set the color of your QR code by clicking on the Color tab and selecting the color you require, and then click OK. You will now have a QR code loaded into your cursor to drag out in your document. (*Note:* If you select a frame in your document prior to creating the QR code, the code image will be placed into that frame.) You can make it as large or small as you would like. If you want to make a change to the link, just Right-click on the QR code, and you'll be taken back to the Generate QR Code dialog. Change the weblink and/or color, and click OK. You'll actually see the pattern change in your QR code to show that it has accepted the change.

I use InDesign's Presentation mode all the time when I'm giving presentations. It allows you to view only your document, without guides, columns, bleed, panels, or the application frame. It can be used with single- or multi-page documents. When you're working with a single page, Presentation mode is good for viewing the document without the clutter of the application frame, panels, or guides. For multi-page documents, it's great to use this as a replacement for something like Keynote or PowerPoint. To enable presentation mode, press **Shift-W**. This gives you a full-screen view of your document. To scroll through a multi-page document, just press the up and down arrow keys, or click with your mouse to go forward a slide (or page) and Shift-click to go back a slide. Once you get used to this, you can get really creative, and it's more flexible for creating great presentations than the standard apps.

TIP: CHANGE THE COLOR OF THE BACKGROUND BORDER
When you're in Presentation mode, you may not like the black background border. Want it to be white or gray, instead? In this full-screen mode, just hit **G** for gray, **W** for white, or **B** for black.

?How Do I... Find Cool Easter Eggs #1: Alien Invasion (Fun)?

This is a fun one, and it serves no purpose other than to inform you that this exists and looks very 1990s clipart-ish. To see our title alien visitor in InDesign just do the following (you will never get these minutes back in your life, I warn you now!):

- Go to **File > Print Presets > Define**.
- Click on New to open the New Print Preset dialog and type Friendly Alien into the Name field (you can ignore the actual preset settings; they aren't important).
- Click OK to save your preset, and click OK again to close the Print Presets dialog.
- Now open or create a new blank document and go to **File > Print**, and then change the Print Preset at the top of the dialog to Friendly Alien.
- Click on the large P in the print preview window in the Print dialog, and there's your alien (and those lost minutes I mentioned).

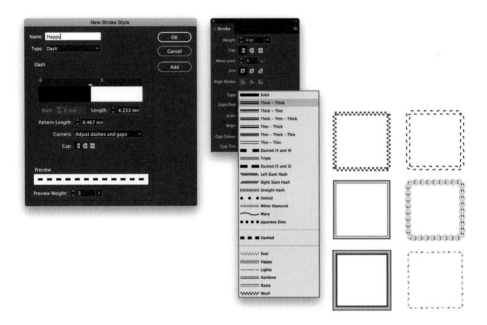

The Strokes panel in InDesign allows you to control and define the kinds of strokes available to you. There are some extra strokes available, but they are not easily seen—you have to create them using a little Easter-egg tomfoolery. Here's how:

- Open the Stroke panel **(Window > Stroke)**.
- Open the panel menu (top-right corner of the panel) and select **Stroke Styles**.
- Click on New to open the New Stroke Style dialog. This is where we can start enabling some hidden stroke styles.
- First, set the Type to **Dash**.
- Now you can create stroke styles called Feet, Happy, Lights, or Woof, just by typing those words into the Name field. You don't need to change any of the stroke settings—just name them, with the correct spelling, and click OK. You can also create Rainbow or Rasta stripes by changing the Type to **Stripe** and typing in Rainbow or Rasta.
- Click OK again to close the Stroke Styles dialog, and your new stroke styles will now be listed in the Stroke panel's Type pop-up menu.

Now you've created your new strokes, and you can test them out by applying them to some of your shapes. Change the stroke size to make the design more visible.

How Do I... Alphabetize My Menus (Cool Easter Egg #3)?

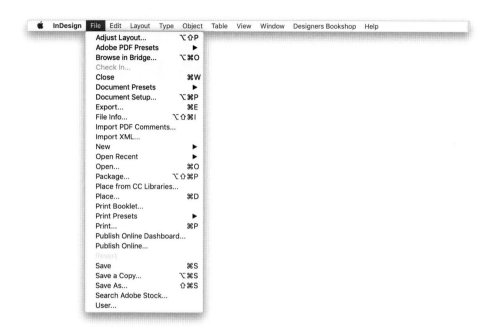

This isn't so much an Easter egg; it's just a cool little feature you may not know about, but that's what this book is for, right? To sort a menu alphabetically while working in InDesign, press-and-hold **Command-Option-Shift (PC: Ctrl-Alt-Shift)** and click on any menu. The alphabetization isn't permanent; it only lasts as long as you have that menu open, but it could be useful!

How Do I... Color Code My Menu Items or Make them Invisible (Cool Easter Egg #4)?

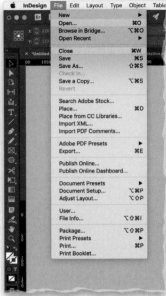

I have learned some new things while writing this book, and I've been reminded of some long-forgotten tips. Here's another one that involves organizing the menus to suit your preferences: you can color code menu items and make them visible or invisible in the menus. Just go to **Edit > Menus**, and you'll be presented with a dialog that lists all of the menus (including application menus, context menus, and panel menus) and menu items in InDesign. Open the Category pop-up menu to select either **Application Menus** or **Context & Panel Menus**. To see the items within each menu listed, click on the arrow to the left of the menu name. Now you can click on the little eye icon to the right of a menu item to turn its visibility off, and click on that same space to turn it back on. You can color code an item by clicking on None (or the name of a color, if one has already been chosen) to enable a pop-up menu, and then selecting whichever color you choose. In the example above, I made "Open" green, and "Close" red. You can save your choices within a new workspace for future use. Don't you just love customization? And rhetorical questions?

How Do I... Find Cool Templates in Adobe Stock?

Sometimes time is against you. Maybe you've picked up a free job or you just need some inspiration. This is where a template will come in handy. The best place to find ready-to-use, professional templates is Adobe Stock. There are hundreds of them, and you can search for them by name. For example, you can type something like "music flyer" into the Adobe Stock search field (in the top-right corner of the InDesign interface), and you'll be taken to the Adobe Stock webpage where you'll be presented with a number of choices. (*Note:* If your InDesign search field says Adobe Help, just click on the little magnifying glass and select **Adobe Stock** from the pop-up menu.) Filter your results to only templates by using the pop-up menu to the left of the search field at the top of the Adobe Stock web page. Then filter them even further to just InDesign templates by clicking on the View filters button on the left side of the web page, and selecting InDesign in the App section. To see a preview of a template, hover over it with your cursor and click on the eye icon in the top-right corner of the image. You can purchase the license for a template and start using it straight away, or simply download and use one of the free ones. I prefer Adobe Stock templates because you can save them right into your CC Libraries folder, and they'll appear in your New Document dialog once you've licensed them.

?How Do I... Find Good Design Resources?

 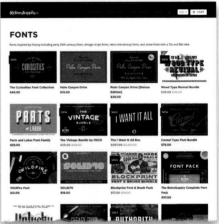

You can find many resources to use in your projects—including things like fonts, images, and vectors—on the internet. Here are some great sites I use to find affordable design resources that can be commercially licensed. Many of these sites offer InDesign-specific resources and have the ability to filter down to INDD files.

Adobe Stock—https://stock.adobe.com
Search and find templates, images, and vectors for your projects.

Retro Supply Co.—https://www.retrosupply.co/collections/fonts
This site offers a really cool selection of fonts and textures for use in your documents. Sign up for the cool free stuff!

Design Cuts—https://www.designcuts.com
This is a fully stocked marketplace of design resources, including fonts.

InDesignSecrets—https://indesignsecrets.com/resources
This site has a ton of really useful free info. Sign up for a yearly membership and get much more, including a subscription to *InDesign Magazine* (PDF) and discounts.

Blurb—https://www.blurb.co.uk/indesign-plugin
Create your own book with an INDD template.

Creative Market—https://creativemarket.com/templates?t=indd
This is one of the leading marketplaces for templates, fonts, images, and textures.

? How Do I... Find Online Training Resources?

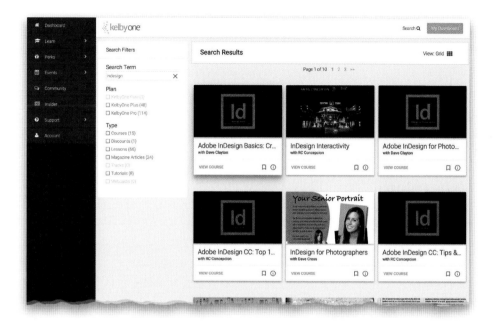

There are many wonderful online training resources that will help you learn new InDesign skills and expand your use of the program. These are some of my favorites:

KelbyOne—https://kelbyone.com
Here you'll find some of my InDesign classes for design projects, as well as many other useful tips-and-tricks classes by RC Concepcion.

LinkedIn Learning (Lynda)—https://www.linkedin.com/learning

Skillshare—https://www.skillshare.com

Creative Live—https://www.creativelive.com/

Udemy—https://www.udemy.com

Terry White—https://www.youtube.com/channel/UC-oYkx9wyeGc6Sh8tkVIaTw

Khara Plicanic—https://kharaplicanic.com/classes

InDesignSecrets—https://www.youtube.com/indesignsecrets

InDesign Magazine **(requires subscription)**—https://indesignsecrets.com/issues

How Do I... Find a List of Keyboard Shortcuts for InDesign?

You can add your own custom set of keyboard shortcuts to InDesign (see page 24), but after a while you may start to wonder how are you going to remember them all. Luckily you don't have to! You can find a list of all the keyboard shortcuts in your set by going to **Edit > Keyboard Shortcuts** and clicking on Show Set. Your text editor will launch and display a list of all the keyboard shortcuts. You can print this as a reference if you wish. If you want to view the most up-to-date list of default keyboard shortcuts for InDesign, you can find them all on the Adobe website at: https://helpx.adobe.com/indesign/using/default-keyboard-shortcuts.html

? How Do I... Make Books with Blurb and InDesign?

While InDesign is very powerful itself, Blurb gives you the ability to design a book using their templates. You can upload your book directly to their website and select the style of book, paper, finishing, binding, etc. I have made a couple of books using the Blurb plug-in, and the books were top-class quality. You can also make your book available for purchase on the Blurb website. Go to Blurb.com, select **Design Tools > Adobe InDesign** near the top of the web page, and download the Adobe InDesign plug-in. Once you've installed it (follow the instructions on their website), you will access the Book Creator from InDesign's File menu **(File > Blurb Book Creator)**. In the dialog that opens, click on Create New Book, and you'll be walked through inputting your book info, and then onto the template section where you begin creating. It's great fun and a good way to get your photos printed for posterity! (*Note:* There's also a Blurb plug-in for Lightroom for all the Lightroom users out there!)

? How Do I... Create Grids with Grid Calculator Pro Edition (Requires License)?

 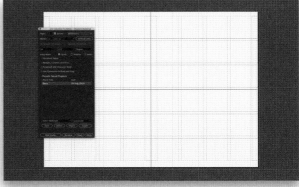

Although the ability to create grids and guides is already available in InDesign, a grid system is more about layout. Grid Calculator is a plug-in I found from DesignersBookshop.com that helps you set out a grid system to assist with your design layout. It is an absolute gem of a find! I contacted the owner, Abraham Georges, to get more info about the plug-in and he is an expert when it comes to working with grid systems. He created this plug-in in 2009 to create layouts that can be very complex. Some of the best designers in the world, including Erik Spiekermann, have been involved in developing the software. I really do like this plug-in and I use it often to lay out complex pages. Clients who already use this tool include: Adidas, American Apparel, HBO, MetaDesign, Forever 21, Forsman & Bodenfors, and Wedge & Lever, to name a few. To download the plug-in, just visit the website: www.gridcalculator.com. (*Note:* There is also a version for Photoshop and Illustrator.) Sign up and subscribe monthly or yearly, and then follow the download instructions. Once the plug-in is installed, you'll need to activate it with the supplied key, and it will then be available under **InDesign (PC: Edit) > Designers Bookshop**. When you select the plug-in from the menu, you'll be guided through a couple of info dialogs before the setup dialog appears. I recommend you check out the available online help and the Designers Bookshop YouTube channel (https://www.youtube.com/user/DesignersBookshop) to get a handle on all the functions.

How Do I... Make Fonts for InDesign in Adobe Photoshop or Illustrator?

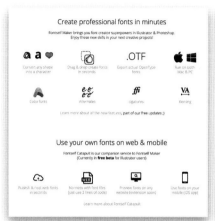

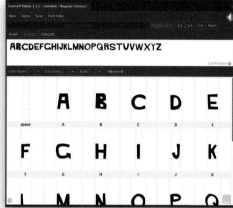

Fontself is not an InDesign plug-in, but it is a cool plug-in for Photoshop and Illustrator that enables you to create your own fonts for use in InDesign. I have been using Fontself for about three years now and it just keeps getting better. When I want a specific font for a project—such as the typeface used on *Photograph Like a Thief*, by Glyn Dewis (Rocky Nook, 2017)—I draw it out in Illustrator and use the Fontself app to create a bespoke font that I am then able to use in InDesign. It's great fun to make your own fonts, and it's even better that you can use them in lots of different apps, not just the Adobe apps. Visit http://fontself.refr.cc/daveclayton to get 10 percent off your purchase.

Index

F

facing pages, 41
file
    information, 49
    location saved, 49
    open recent, 21
    save, 244–247
    size, 49
fill color
    apply, 140
    default, 142
    stroke, swap with, 141
font
    activate, 85, 88
    Adobe Fonts, 85, 258
    change, 84, 89
    Creative Cloud, 88
    custom, 279
    DDC Hardware, 192
    default, set, 112
    Extensis Tools, 265, 266
    favorite, mark as, 86
    filter, 86
    find, 88, 266
    Fontself, 279
    global change, 89
    missing, 88
    organize, 265
    package files, 257
    plug-in for font management, 265
    search document for, 266
    similar, finding, 87
    Suitcase Fusion, 265, 266
Fontself, 279
frame fitting options, 173, 174
frames, 51–81
    align, 77, 78
    auto text frame, 59
    combine frames, 70
    convert, 71
    corners, 67–69
    create, 53, 73
    custom, 73, 74
    distribution, 79
    fit to content, 62, 173, 174
    frame fitting options, 61, 173, 174
    graphic, 52, 53
    grid, create, 63, 64
    hide, 186
    in port/out port, 105
    lines, draw, 76
    linked text frames, 105
    move with content, 119
    multiples, create, 63, 64
    Pathfinder options, 70
    paths, 75
    Pen Tool, create with, 74
    Pencil Tool, create with, 72
    replace content, 60
    rotate, 65, 66
    scale, 65, 66
    scale with content, 62
    shear, 65, 66
    spacing between, 79
    styles, object, 127, 128
    text, 52, 53, 58, 59, 91
    threaded text frames, 105
    tools, 53
    transform, 65, 66
    unassigned, 52
full screen, view document, 19, 44

G

glyphs, 98
gradient
    across objects, 165
    apply, 164
    create new, 163
    save as swatch, 164
    type, 109
Gradient panel, 163
graphics. *See* images
grid
    columns and rows, 17
    document, 16

T

Type Tool, 53, 58
  auto text frame, 59
  shortcut, 114

W

warning icon, 184
web, publish for, 259
width, document, 45
word count, check, 93
Word document, insert, 100
workspace
  Application Frame, 11
  customize, 8
  reset, 8
  save setup, 8
  "Start," 5
  reset, 8

Z

zoom in/out, 20